Baedeker's

SEYCHELLES

Imprint
72 illustrations, 4 drawings, 1 town plan, 1 special map, 1 large map at end of the book

Original German text: Dr Eckhard Supp
Editorial work: Baedeker (Gisela Bockamp)
English language edition: Alec Court

General direction: Dr Peter Baumgarten, Baedeker Stuttgart

Cartography: Gert Oberländer, Munich
Ordnance Survey, Southampton (large map of the Seychelles)

Source of Illustrations: Air Seychelles (1), Historia-Photo (1), Michael Adams Pictures (1), Motiv-Bildagentur: Reif (4); Witzovsky (7), Nahm (1), Seychelles Tourist Office (4), Supp (51), Ullstein-Bilderdienst (1), Camera Press Ltd. (1), Financial Times (1)

English translation: Wendy Bell

Following the tradition established by Karl Baedeker in 1844, sights of particular interest and hotels and restaurants of particular quality are distinguished by either one or two asterisks.

Only a selection of hotels, restaurants and shops can be given; no reflection is implied therefore on establishments not included.

In a time of rapid change it is difficult to ensure that all the information given is entirely accurate and up-to-date, and the possibility of error can never be entirely eliminated. Although the publishers can accept no responsibility for inaccuracies and omissions, they are always grateful for corrections and suggestions for improvement.

1st English edition 1992

© Baedeker Stuttgart
Original German edition

© 1992 Jarrold and Sons Limited
English language edition worldwide

© 1992 The Automobile Association
United Kingdom and Ireland

US and Canadian edition
Prentice Hall Press

Distributed in the United Kingdom by the Publishing Division of the Automobile Association, Fanum House, Basingstoke, Hampshire RG21 2EA

Licensed user:
Mairs Geographischer Verlag GmbH & Co., Ostfildern-Kemnat bei Stuttgart

The name *Baedeker* is a registered trade mark
A CIP catalogue record of this book is available from the British Library

Printed in Italy by G. Canale & C.S.p.A – Borgaro T.se –Turin

ISBN USA and Canada 0–13–059536–5
    UK 0 7495 0558 3

Contents

The Principal Sights at a Glance

Preface

This guide to the Seychelles is one of the new generation of Baedeker guides.

These guides, illustrated throughout in colour, are designed to meet the needs of the modern traveller. They are quick and easy to consult, with the principal places of interest described in alphabetical order, and the information is presented in a format that is both attractive and easy to follow.

The subject of this guide is the Seychelles Islands in the Indian Ocean – from the much-visited granite islands in the north-east to the coral islands and atolls in the south and south-west.

The guide is in three parts. The first part gives a general account of the islands, their characteristics, climate, flora and fauna, underwater life, the state and population, economy, history, famous people, culture and art. A brief selection of quotations and a number of suggested itineraries for car drives and walks provide a transition to the second part, in which the places and features of tourist interest – islands with beautiful beaches, and attractive villages, appealing scenery, animals and plants, are described, The third part contains a variety of practical information. Both the sights and the practical information are listed in alphabetical order.

The new Baedeker guides are noted for their concentration on essentials and their convenience of use. They contain numerous specially drawn plans and colour illustrations; and at the end of the book is a large map, to assist the user in locating the various places described in the "A to Z" section of the guide.

Facts and Figures

In the course of the last few hundred years the Seychelles have been under the dominion of first the French and then the British. As a result alternative spellings have arisen for the names of some of the islands. While in practice the words "Island" or "Île" are often dropped in ordinary conversation ("North" being used for "North Island" or "Aride" for "Île Aride") the full names of the islands are given in the main headings of the "Seychelles from A to Z" section of this guide.

Explanatory note

General

The guide covers the islands and island groups in the western Indian Ocean collectively known as the "Seychelles" (formerly "Séchelles").

Area covered

The Seychelles extend between latitude 3°43′ and 10°8′S and between longitude 46°10′ and 56°20′E. The principal island, Mahé, lies some 1580km east of Mombasa (Kenya), 930km north of Madagascar, 2800km southwest of Bombay (India) and 2260km south of Aden (Yemen). Aldabra Atoll, the most westerly island in the group, is just 650km from the coast of Tanzania; Farquhar, the southernmost island, lies only 400km off the northern tip of Madagascar. The islands in the Amirantes are some 300km from

Location

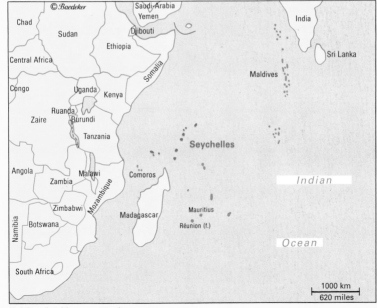

◀ A beach with coconut palms

General

Mahé, the Farquhar and Aldabra groups some 800 and 1100km distant respectively.

Land and sea areas

The territory of the Seychelles (as they are now called even in French) is officially made up of 115 named islands and atolls together with a large number of islets and reefs, a total land area of 445sq.km. They lie scattered over a sea area of almost 400,000sq.km. If the Seychelles exclusive economic maritime zone is also taken into account this sea area increases to over a million sq.km.

Origin of the name

Before being taken over by the French and later the British the Seychelles were known in the western world by the Portuguese names "os sete irmas" ("the seven sisters") or "os irmãos" ("the brothers"). On the oldest maps showing the Seychelles – or at least islands assumed to be them – the principal island is called "Y. Rana". Arab sources dating from the 14th c.

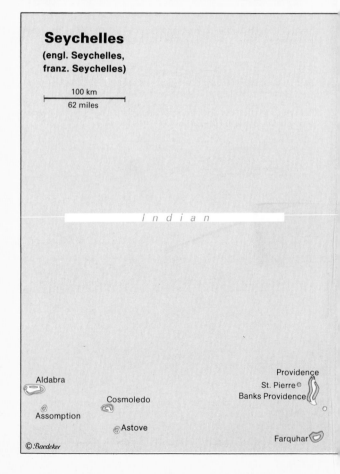

Seychelles
(engl. Seychelles,
franz. Seychelles)

100 km
62 miles

I n d i a n

Providence
St. Pierre ○
Banks Providence

Aldabra

Cosmoledo

Assomption

Astove

Farquhar

© *Baedeker*

also mention a group of islands called the "zarin" ("the sisters") in this part of the Indian Ocean. The name Aldabra probably derives directly from the Arabic expression "al khadra" meaning "the green one".

Two years after having christened it the "Île d'Abondance, Lazare Picault, on his second voyage of discovery in 1744, renamed Mahé after Bertrand François Mahé de Labourdonnais, the then Governor of the French "Île de France" (now Mauritius), who had commissioned and equipped Picault's expedition. The archipelago as a whole was christened the "Îles de Labourdonnais".

In 1756 Captain Nicolas Morphey renamed the islands "Séchelles" after the French Contrôleur des Finances Jean-Moreau de Séchelles, Louis XV's Minister of Finance and later Intendant of the Compagnie des Indes. Under British rule this was later anglicised in the 19th c. to "Seychelles".

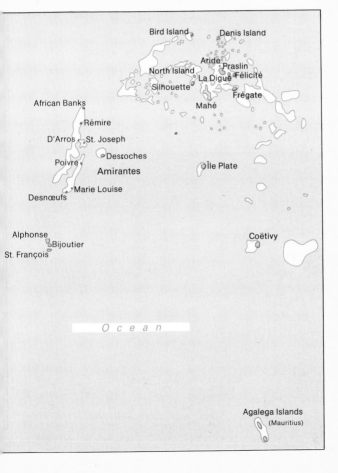

The Nature of the Islands

Granite islands and coral islands

Island groups

The Seychelles are made up of six large island groups and two further islands which stand alone. Forming one group are the granite islands of the so-called Seychelles or Mahé Plateau, with which are included (by virtue of their position on the edge of this underwater tableland) two coral islands, Denis Island and Bird Island. That leaves the coral islands of the Amirantes, Alphonse and Farquhar groups, the Aldabra and the Cosmoledo Atolls together with the smaller islands around them, and the two lone islands, Île Plate and Coëtivy (see map pp 10/11).

Granite islands

Surrounding Mahé are the 41 granite islands of the Mahé Plateau (known collectively as the "Inner Islands"). In addition to Mahé itself (152.5sq.km plus 1.24sq.km of reclaimed land) they include Praslin (37.56sq.km), Silhouette (19.95sq.km), La Digue (10.10sq.km), Curieuse Island (2.86sq.km), Félicité (2.68sq.km), Frégate (2.19sq.km), Ste Anne (2.19sq.km), North (2.01sq.km), Marianne (0.95sq.km), Grande Sœur (0.84sq.km), Thérèse (0.74sq.km), Aride (0.68sq.km), Conception (0.60sq.km) and Petite Sœur (0.34sq.km), also Cousin (0.29sq.km) and Cousine (0.26sq.km).

These "Inner Islands" divide in fact into four groups: Mahé and its satellites, the two islands Silhouette and North, the Praslin-La Digue group, and finally Frégate and its neighbours. The submarine plateau on which they stand, roughly circular in shape, extends for about 400km around Mahé. Some 20,000sq.km in area the flat top of this granite pedestal is only between 30 and 75m below sea level. Around its perimeter the sea floor falls away abruptly to a depth of 1800m. The Seychelles or Mahé Plateau is part of the so-called Mascarene Ridge, a sort of underwater mountain chain

Granite rocks at Anse Lazio (Praslin)

A coral island in the Indian Ocean

which stretches in a north–south direction from the Seychelles to the islands of Mauritius and Réunion.

The rock formations of the islands of the Mahé Plateau are unique. Nowhere else in the world can such an abundance of granite islands be found on such a scale, lying in the midst of an ocean thousands of kilometres from the mainland of the surrounding continents. The particular type of rock varies from island to island. While grey or grey-brown granite predominates on Mahé and a pale grey gneiss is typical of Ste Anne, the peaks of Praslin and La Digue consist largely of red rock. And while the granite on Praslin is shot through with veins of almost pure quartz, the syenite found on La Digue contains virtually no quartz at all.

The coral islands and atolls, amalgamated with the Mahé group only in the years between 1903 and 1932, make up a second geological family of islands in the Seychelles. Among them are Denis Island (1.43sq.km) and Bird Island (1.01sq.km) which, although coral, are considered part of the main Seychelles group on account of their geographical position on the northern edge of the Mahé Plateau.

Coral islands

The remaining coral islands (known as the "Outer Islands") divide up into five principal groups and atolls: the Amirantes (6.61sq.km in land area) together with St Joseph (1.22sq.km) and Poivre Atoll (2.48sq.km) and also the African Banks (0.30sq.km); Aldabra Atoll (153.80sq.km) and the small island of Assomption (1.71sq.km); Cosmoledo Atoll (5.09sq.km) together with the island of Astove (6.61sq.km); the Alphonse group (1.74sq.km) with St François Atoll (0.17sq.km) and Bijoutier (0.07sq.km); finally the Farquhar (7.99sq.km) and Providence group (3.95sq.km). Also coral are the two islands which stand alone, Coëtivy (9.31sq.km) and Plate (0.54sq.km).

There are two different types of coral island. On the one hand there are islands such as Denis, Bird, Plate, Coëtivy and the Amirantes, comprised of

13

coral sandbanks most of which have formed in the shallow waters above a submarine ridge. The majority of these are no more than 3000 years old. On the other hand there are the coral reefs and atolls – circular reefs which have grown up around the rims of submerged volcanic craters. These, like Aldabra Atoll, are found in waters of greater depth and some are 150,000 years old or even older. When the encircling reef becomes broken up into separate islets, narrow passages form linking the formerly enclosed lagoon with the sea.

On most coral islands, between the surface sand and the limestone bedrock (composed of the skeletons of dead coral) a "bubble" of fresh water is trapped, "floating" on the saline groundwater beneath. It forms as a result of rainwater percolating downwards which, because of the slow diffusion of salt and freshwater, mixes only very gradually with the water from the sea.

Scenery of the islands

The Seychelles, and in particular the islands of the Mahé group, correspond almost exactly with the popular idea of an exotic holiday island. Superb and often near-empty beaches, a warm, crystal-clear sea with – especially on the east coast, where the equatorial current from the southeast ensures a supply of fresh, warm water – extensive coral banks just below the surface, tropical vegetation with palm groves and brightly coloured flowers, the bizarre rock formations of the granite islands with their precipitous massifs, the little villages and the fishing boats on the beach; all this, with the secluded and for the most part sparsely inhabited coral islands, makes for a leisure and nature holiday which few other holiday destinations can match. The rocky massifs with their deep ravines and cliffs jutting into the sea consist of polished granite, mainly grey, grey-brown or reddish in colour. The beaches, with the exception of those on the northwest coast of Mahé, are mostly situated in little bays called "anses", sheltered by rocks and with a screen of tropical vegetation on the landward side.

Most popular with holidaymakers is the island of Mahé, noted for its steep mountain massif. The Morne Seychellois rises above sea level to a height of 905m, leaving room for only a narrow coastal strip. The island has little cultivatable land, what there is being frequently broken up by swampland and mangrove forest.
Other favourite resorts are the islands of Praslin and La Digue which, in contrast to Mahé, have the gentlest of landscapes (the highest points being only 367m and 333m respectively).

The rest of the granite and coral islands also have much to recommend them, particularly to holidaymakers who prefer to get away from the tourist crowd in a natural landscape rich in rare plants, birds and sealife. The long white beaches of Denis and Bird, the densely wooded Frégate, the coral reefs of Desroches; all offer a chance to experience nature with an immediacy no longer possible in Europe or in many other areas of the world favoured by tourists.

Many of the more remote coral islands however are nature reserves or, being privately owned, are not open to tourists. Access to them is sometimes completely prohibited or requires special permission. In recent years the Seychelles government has approved development programmes for a number of these coral islands; mostly small-scale commercial and tourist ventures are planned. The islands of Desroches, D'Arros, Marie-Louise, Rémire, Alphonse, Astove, Farquhar and Coëtivy already have runways used by small aircraft belonging to the Air Seychelles and the Island Development Commission; the other islands can only be reached by boat.

Origin of the islands

The granite Mahé Plateau dates from the pre-Cambrian period, having come into existence c. 650 million years ago. By contrast, the darker

A beach near the Sheraton Hotel (Mahé)

granite-like syenite of the rock formations on Silhouette and North was only formed during the Tertiary period, i.e. less than 60 million years ago. It is generally assumed today that the Seychelles came into being as a group of islands more than 200 million years ago when the primeval land mass of "Gondwanaland" broke up into the continents of South America, Africa, Asia and Australia. For a considerable time land bridges survived at points where the new continents had been connected, before gradually sinking beneath the sea. The legend of "Lemuria", a mythical land allegedly swallowed up by the sea, may have originated from these geological events.

With continuing continental drift the land bridges between Africa and India eventually disappeared and the islands in the Indian Ocean situated between latitudes 4° and 27°S are now all the traces that remain. The granite islands of the Seychelles are thought to have originally been part of the drifting land mass of India. It was only later that Madagascar split off from Africa and Ceylon from India.

The islands of Mauritius and Réunion, the Comoros, and the Aldabra and Cosmoledo Atolls owe their origin to the increased volcanic activity along the fault lines in East Africa and the Indian Ocean. On the other hand, the Maldives for example, were created by a slow build up of banks of coral from the sea floor.

During the last ice age when the sea level was lower by almost 100m, the Mahé Plateau probably appeared as an uninterrupted land surface – the depth of water over it today hardly varies from between 60 and 75m.

The Indian Ocean

The Indian Ocean is the third largest of the earth's oceans and accounts for some 20% of the earth's total ocean surface area. Depending on whether

The Nature of the Islands

At Anse Consolation (Praslin)

the Antarctic Sea is counted part of it (on which opinions differ) its surface area amounts to *c.* 45 or 72 million sq.km. It is about half as big as the Pacific Ocean and somewhat smaller than the Atlantic. It extends from the line which divides it from the Atlantic at Cape Agulhas (longitude 20°E) to its boundary with the Pacific at Tasmania (longitude 147°E). It reaches to latitude 30°N (in the Persian Gulf and the Red Sea), and to latitude 70°S.

At its deepest it is 8500m. Access is via the Strait of Malacca between Indonesia and Malaysia and the Timor Sea between Indonesia and Australia, round the Cape of Good Hope in South Africa or through Suez in the extreme north-west.

For political and ideological reasons the Indian Ocean is sometimes also referred to as the Afro-Asiatic Ocean or the Indonesian Ocean. In recent years the abbreviation "Indic" has come into use – mirroring the more familiar "Pacific" and "Atlantic".

Island chains

The islands of the Indian Ocean form three great chains. The first of these, almost a circle, stretches from the Amirantes, through the Seychelles, the Cargados and Mauritius, to Réunion. The second, spanning a distance of more than 2300km, runs north–south across the equator. Formed of coral banks it embraces the Laccadives, Minicoy, the Amindives, the Maldives and the Chagos Islands with Diego Garcia. The island groups lying between Burma and Sumatra make up the third chain which includes the Cocos, Andaman and Nicobar Islands.

Economic importance

One third of the world's population lives on the perimeter of the "Indic", of which almost three-quarters inhabit the Indian subcontinent and 16% are in South-East Asia. The economic significance of the ocean lies first and foremost in its raw material deposits and those of the countries which border it. The region possesses two thirds of the world's oil reserves (on which Japan depends for 90% and Germany for 62% of their supplies),

16

60% of its uranium deposits, 40% of its gold and 98% of its diamonds. Other important raw materials found here are thorium, coal, iron, copper, manganese, tin, bauxite, nickel, chromium, asbestos, vanadium, jute and rubber. Many of these raw materials lie underwater on and beneath the extensive continental shelf which constitutes almost 5% of the ocean floor. Their extraction poses considerable ecological and demographic problems for the region. Seawater pollution in particular – the result of population growth in the coastal areas and a massive increase in tanker traffic – has become a major environmental concern.

In addition to their mineral wealth the countries on the rim of the Indian Ocean account for one fifth of the world's land suitable for agriculture. The sea itself is stocked with an estimated 15 million tonnes of fish supporting an annual catch of 2.5 million tonnes.

Despite this wealth of natural resources the countries of the "Indic" are still relatively underdeveloped from an industrial point of view, with only a handful of the 47 states (India, South Africa, Pakistan, Singapore, Australia and Indonesia in particular) boasting an industrial infrastructure on any significant scale. The region's trade is still very much determined by economic relations with countries of the so-called "first world" – trade internal to the Indian Ocean region itself accounts for only about 10% of total volume.

Of the world's three great oceans it is the smallest which can claim the longest history as far as economic and political importance are concerned. The Atlantic assumed real global significance only in the 18th c., and the Pacific only in the 20th c. For the major powers of the time however, the Indian Ocean already had an important role in trade and communications as early as the 15th c. Prior to the discovery of America it was the ocean with the most navigation and there was a correspondingly lively degree of cultural interchange across its waters – which is why, for example, so many expressions from Indian languages have found their way into African Somalia.

History

The importance of the "Indic" actually dates back much further. Under the Pharaohs the Egyptians had begun to navigate the ocean as long ago as 2300 B.C. From the time of Ramses I's son Sethi, the main route connecting the Mediterranean Sea with the Far East – which was later, in 1869, to become the Suez Canal – was rebuilt at least four times, before finally the "gateway" to the Indian Ocean was allowed to silt up by the caliphate in an attempt to stem the influx of Christian "infidels". In their quest for gold, silver, ivory and slaves the Phoenicians ventured as far as Sri Lanka and Malaysia, and from the end of the 7th c. Arabs dhows were sailing to Indonesia and even China. As early as 851 Arab mariners were already equipped with sailing directions for the Indian Ocean, compiled by one of their number called Suleiman.

Being relatively constant and predictable throughout the year (blowing for six months from one direction and then six from the other), the winds in the Indian Ocean are favourable to marine commerce no matter what the state of maritime technology. This factor was to prove of crucial importance to Europe, especially after the defeat of the Mongolians by the Chinese in 1370 and the subsequent closure of the overland trade routes between Europe and China. At first, when after the fall of Constantinople the Ottoman Empire gained control of the sea routes and with it a monopoly on Far East trade, Europe's rulers and new middle class had no option but to pay the enormous sums demanded for the much sought after spices and aromatics from the Orient. Later however the determination of the spice-importing countries to break the Arab stranglehold on trade (to which the Venetians were party) and to exploit for themselves the vast potential for commercial profit, brought into being the Age of Discovery. First the Portuguese and then the Dutch opened up the sea routes round the southern tip of Africa, the latter quickly establishing their own monopoly of the spice trade. Prior to that the Chinese had for a time almost dominated the Indian Ocean. Between 1405 and 1432 they embarked on seven expeditions

Navigation

against the eastern and western shores of the "Indic", sending into battle fleets of up to 60 war-junks crewed by 28,000 men.

In more recent centuries the Indian Ocean became the plaything of the French and British colonial powers. Indeed prior to 1900 the British enjoyed such a marked supremacy in the region that the Ocean was referred to as the "British Lake". The British presence ended only in 1971 when the then Labour government abruptly decided to dispense with any military bases "east of Suez". France still maintains a small but strategically significant presence in the region (Réunion, Mayotte) while also working actively to keep alive French cultural influence in many of the islands (Seychelles, Mauritius).

Developments in the 20th c.

After the Second World War most of the countries bordering the Indian Ocean gained independence from their colonial masters: India, Pakistan, Burma and Ceylon in 1947 and 1948, Indonesia 1949, Malaysia 1957, Singapore 1963, Somalia 1960, Tanganyika (now united with Zanzibar and Pemba as Tanzania) 1961, Kenya 1963, South Yemen (now part of Yemen) 1967, Mauritius 1968 and finally the Seychelles in 1976. In 1963 rising political turbulence among the non-aligned nations, in the wake of the Indo-Chinese border conflict of 1962, was one of the main reasons for the dispatch of the US 7th Fleet to the region. In 1970, in the face of an increasing Soviet naval presence in the area, the US Congress voted resources for the construction of a naval base on Diego Garcia, begun two years later. The events in Iran and Afganistan as well as those in Iraq have in recent years once again drastically altered the geo-political significance and role of the Indian Ocean.

Alfred T. Mahan, an American admiral living at the end of the 19th c., observed that the Indian Ocean is the key to seven seas and that in the 21st c. the Earth's fate will be decided on its waters.

Climate

General

Occupying a position close to the equator the Seychelles, and the Mahé group in particular, enjoy a tropical maritime climate which shows little variation throughout the year. Such marginal differences as there are make it possible nevertheless to distinguish three basic "seasons": the cooler, drier period from May to October when the south-east monsoon blows, sometimes quite strongly; the wetter, hotter months of the north-west monsoon from December to March; and the transitional months of April/May and October/November.

Temperature

The mean annual temperature on Mahé is 26.6°C, with an average maximum of 30.3°C and an average minimum of 25°C. Temperatures as high as 31° or 32°C are experienced mainly in April and May, during the calm conditions which prevail between the two monsoons; the lowest daily temperatures (c. 27°C) occur in July and August. The highest and lowest temperatures recorded are 34° and 19.8°C respectively.

Sea temperature is a constant 26° to 30°C the whole year round, guaranteeing excellent bathing at all seasons. Humidity levels are also very stable, and at 75 to 81% are lower and more comfortable than in other tropical holiday areas. The sun shines for an average of seven hours a day, again with little variation through the year.

Rainfall

The average rainfall of the Seychelles is c. 1500 to 2200mm a year, of which much the greater part falls on the hilly granite islands – in contrast to the flatter coral islands which are often less than a metre above sea level. Precipitation is highest on the island of Silhouette, but up to 4000mm can also fall at altitude on Mahé. While the annual rainfall is not evenly distributed (most falling in the months from December to April) hours of sunshine per day remain fairly constant. This is because, although the rain is certainly heavier in those months, it never lasts for more than an hour or two. Wet weather persisting for several days or a week is quite exceptional.

The Seychelles – with the exception of the most southerly island groups of Farquhar, Cosmoledo and Aldabra – lie outside the cyclone belt and so are spared the severe tropical storms which periodically afflict Mauritius, Réunion and other subtropical and tropical tourist areas. Very occasionally Mahé and other islands in the main group may be affected by weak secondary depressions. There is only one recorded instance of a violent cyclone causing major damage and loss of life and that was in 1862. Monsoons

Winds in the Seychelles, as in most of the "Indic" basin, are dominated by the monsoons. These can blow with the same strength and from the same direction for four months at a time, from the south-east during the European summer and the north-west in the months from December to March. It was the reliability of these monsoon winds that gave rise to the term "trade winds", making possible and establishing the rhythm of trade in the Indian Ocean at a time when the arts of sailing and navigation were still in their infancy.

The most widely accepted explanation for the south-east monsoon is the persistence of an area of high pressure in the southern Indian Ocean from April to October. During summer in the northern hemisphere the hot air masses over the continent of Asia rise, creating a "sink" into which air is drawn from the south. This steady stream of air is deflected to the north-west by the rotation of the earth, thus becoming the south-east monsoon. The south-east monsoon is relatively cool because heat is taken out of the atmosphere through the evaporation of sea water.

In the months of November/December to March, when the sun has moved back into the southern hemisphere, the mechanism is reversed, resulting in the north-west monsoon. The north-west monsoon is much less reliable and generally weaker than its south-eastern counterpart, and brings with it more rain. In the interval between the two monsoons, when the sun is more or less over the equator, almost total calm prevails. At this time of year the sea is also at its calmest and hence clearest, offering ideal conditions for diving, deep sea angling, snorkelling and swimming.

Thanks to their heavier rainfall the hilly granite islands in the Seychelles group are blessed with ample water. At one time it was allowed to run away unchecked, flowing quickly over the steep rock faces and down the short, deep ravines into the sea. As a result there were problems with the water supply, especially during extended periods of drought. In Mahé a number of dams have now been built to regulate the supply. On Praslin, which obtains its water largely from rain collected in the Vallée de Mai, hotels can still sometimes experience shortages in May and June. On La Digue too, where supplies are drawn from the ground water, there is scarcity from time to time. Water supply

Given their substantially lower rainfall the coral islands can depend on rainwater reservoirs only for their drinking water. For other uses supplies are drawn from the freshwater "bubble" floating on the saline waters below the sand. It is because this ground water is still comparatively salty that hot water is limited on many islands (e.g. Bird and Denis); the high salinity would very quickly corrode any heating installations. As yet there are very few sea water desalination plants (although there are some – at the new Bungalow Hotel on Desroches for example).

Weather Table*

Month	Average temperature max. °C	min. °C	Rainfall (mm)	Average hours of sunshine (per day)
January	29.8	24.2	387	4.7
February	30.4	24.7	283	6.2
March	30.9	24.9	177	6.8
April	31.3	25,1	186	7.6
May	30.6	25,5	107	8.4
June	29.2	24.8	61	7.7
July	28.3	24.1	64	7.5
August	28.5	24.1	101	7.5
September	29.0	24,3	120	7.6
October	29.6	24.4	216	7.1
November	30.1	24.0	217	6.7
December	29.9	23.9	296	5.5
Temperature (Average annual)	30.3	25.0		
Sunshine (Average daily)				7.0
Rainfall (total)			2215	

*1972 to 1988 mean values, recorded at Point La Rue international airport.

Plants

General

The flora of the Seychelles is really quite limited. In fact there are only about 400 different plant species, but these are characterised by a great variety of shapes and colours. Of special interest are the 81 plants endemic to the islands, i.e. unique to the Seychelles and in many cases to only one or two of the islands.

The chance to experience nature in all its richness is one of the Seychelles' greatest holiday attractions, complementing the sea and the sun. Birds and other creatures in their native habitats, rare plants, fish, and a whole luxuriant world under the sea, are all part of the natural setting of any visit to the islands. On the uninhabited coral islands in particular the wildlife is seldom shy and can often be observed from very close quarters.

Nature conservation

Particularly in recent years the government of the Republic of the Seychelles has come to recognise the need for systematic nature conservation and – partly in co-operation with or on the initiative of the international organisations – has created a large number of nature reserves (including national parks). This policy is closely linked with the attempt to develop a "nature friendly", close-to-nature tourist industry, which involves limiting the total number of tourist beds and opening up the outer islands to holidaymakers only very gradually and with great care.

Guided nature tours feature among the excursions available to visitors on those islands which are accessible – e.g. Cousin Island with its teeming birdlife and in the Vallée de Mai on Praslin. On Mahé the tourist office has signposted a number of nature trails.

Indigenous vegetation

In earlier times the granite islands of the Seychelles were covered with a tropical jungle of tall trees and dense foliage. From the 18th and 19th c.

onwards however, profound changes to the whole eco-system wrought by settlement have resulted in native plants being replaced almost entirely by new varieties. Only high up in the hills and on some of the outlying islands is it still possible to find anything reminiscent of the original vegetation. Botanical studies of the period before colonisation have distinguished four vegetation zones on the granite islands: first the large tracts of ground over which coastal swamps and mangrove forests predominated; next, on higher ground up to an altitude of c. 300m, dense woodland with trees as tall as 40m; then another wooded belt of smaller trees (with orchids), extending to 600m above sea level; finally, near the summits, an area of still lower growth (up to 15m). It was at this fourth level that plant varieties typical of tropical rainforest (e.g. the very characteristic carnivorous pitcher plant) were found.

On Mahé the mangrove forests, which at one time formed a continuous belt (particularly in the bay of Victoria, extending all the way from Pointe Conan to Pointe La Rue), are nowadays confined to quite small areas (mainly around Port Launay and south of Mont Fleuri on the road from Victoria to the airport). Called mangliers, and so striking in appearance, the mangroves have survived best on the almost untouched Aldabra Atoll. There are four main types – Manglier hauban (Rhizophora mucronata), Manglier jaune (Ceriops sagal), Manglier gros poumon (Brugiera gymnorhiza) and Manglier fleur (Sonneratia caseolaris). Common to all is the ability to flourish in the shallow salt water swamps along the island shores, sustained by meagre amounts of freshwater from the streams and small river courses.

Mangrove forest

Like the decline of the mangrove swamps at the coast, the number of native plants in the inland zones has also decreased significantly during the last 200 years. Colonisation proved highly detrimental to the islands' eco-systems. Within a period of only 25 years precious woods suffered intensive and indiscrimate felling (ships of up to 300 tonnes were built in the Seychelles); slaves freed in the 1840s left the plantations on the coast and burned down woodland in the intermediate and high altitude zones to create fields and gardens for cultivation. Later on cinnamon became rampant, almost completely supplanting the remaining indigenous vegetation. As if this were not enough, introduced species and wild varieties were allowed to spread rapidly – albizzia, wild pineapple, black pepper and then tea – in some cases becoming a major nuisance.

Present vegetation

Today the vegetation typical of the low lying areas along the coasts is relatively uniform up to a height of c. 300m. Most common of all is the coconut palm (*Cocos nucifera*), plantations of which were once the mainstay of the Seychelles economy but which has since spread out of hand. These palms are known to have existed on the islands as long ago as 1609 and still flourish on almost all the cultivated land (amounting to a quarter of the area of the Seychelles). On the coral islands in particular coconut palms are often the only sort of vegetation. Among other lowland species are the takamaka trees, also known as Alexandrine laurel (*Calophylum inophyllum*) and casuarinas (*Casuarina equisetifolia*). There is uncertainty as to whether these really are indigenous to the islands; their seeds may have been introduced by Indonesian tribes people (assumed to have reached the islands at an early point in their history) or perhaps carried naturally across the vast expanse of ocean. The raffia palm, of Madagascan and East African origin, is another coloniser of the humid coastal strip. With leaves which can grow up to 20m it blooms only once and then dies. At higher levels of the coastal zone indigenous trees are found: bois blanc (*Hernandia ovigera*) and bois rouge (*Noewormia ferruginea*), the once endemic species bois de fer, now reduced to just a dozen specimens, and ironwood (*Veteria seychellarum*) which attains a height of more than 40m. They mix with

Albizzia, a broad-crowned tree

imported species such as eucalyptus (*Eucalyptus sp.*) and albizzia (*Albizzia falcataria*), a fast-growing tree with a large thinly foliated crown which has become typical of the Mahé landscape. Also to be seen is the occasional banyan tree (*Ficus benghalensis*) with its gigantic aerial roots. Its seeds germinate on other plants and end up completely strangling the host. Additionally there are a large number of exotic varieties, i.e. ornamental plants introduced by the settlers. These include flamboyant or flame trees (*Delonix regia*), hibiscus (*Hibiscus sinensis*), bougainvillea (*Bougainvillea spectabilis*), "cat's-tail" (*Acalypha hispida*) and begonias (*Begonia ulmifolia* and *Begonia humilis*).

Growing in the intermediate zone between 300 and 600m are mainly native types of palm, among them the palmiste (*Deckenia nobilis*) from the soft upper butt of which the famous millionaire's salad is prepared, and two varieties of latanias (*Nephrosperma vanhoutteeana* and *Phoenicophorium borsigianum*) which are extremely rare in other parts of the world. Then there are screw pines, called "vacoas" (*Pandanus sp.*), and 40 known specimens of the endemic and famous though less spectacular "jellyfish" tree, which can grow up to 8m tall and has blooms resembling jellyfish. (Botanists have pronounced this an independent variety – *Medusagyne oppositifolia*.) Another equally rare plant found at this altitude is the Wright's gardenia, or bois citron (*Rothmania annae*), already extinct in South America and now thought to survive only on the island of Aride (though its white flowers will also be spotted near the start of the trail up to the "Trois Frères" peak on Mahé Island). At the Seychelles Mission Lodge on the Forêt Noire Road (again on Mahé) are two rows of massive sandragon trees (*Ptecarpus indicus*) below which grow a mixture of cinnamon trees (*Cinnamonum zeylanicum*), the abizzias and latania palms already referred to, a number of different orchids including a wild and an imported variety of vanilla, and finally the strange icaco plum trees (*Crysobalanus*

"Pitcher Plant" (canna liana)

icaco), known here as "coco plums" or "prune de France" (the floury white flesh inside their red fruit is actually rather tasteless).

The third and upper level of vegetation is a typical tropical cloud forest where the smallest of the latania palms can be found. Latania hauban (*Roscheria melanochaetes*) grows only on the summits of hills in Mahé and Silhouette; it reaches a height of 2 to 3m and its trunk is a bare 5cm in diameter.
The most remarkable plant at this altitude is the carnivorous pitcher plant (*Nepenthes pervillei*) which has mainly colonised the bare crags of the granite massifs. Its leaf tendrils are shaped like pitchers, which secrete nectar to attract insects. Once the victim becomes trapped in the sticky secretion the pitcher lid closes and the insect is digested. There is one particular type of mosquito however which is apparently immune, even depositing its eggs to hatch in the plant's digestive juices.

Coco de mer

The coco de mer is the fruit of the Seychelles palm (*Lodoicea maldivica* or *seychellarum*), an endemic plant only found in the Vallée de Mai on Praslin – though one or two can be seen on Curieuse Island and La Digue. With its 50cm long bipartite nut it is the most spectacular plant in the Indian Ocean. The origin of this "double" coconut (shaped like a female backside) remained undiscovered until 1768. Consequently it was a great source of wonder to people wherever it was found washed up by the sea. Around the coasts of India, Ceylon and Indonesia a rich tangle of legend grew up concerning the extraordinary nut which was thought to be the fruit of some gigantic underwater tree (hence the name "coco de mer"). Because of its rarity, the mystery of its origin and its sexually suggestive shape (on account of which aphrodisiacal properties were attributed to it), the coco de mer became one of the most prized commodities in Asia. At one time incredibly high prices were paid to procure one of the rare examples of it and elaborately decorated cocos de mer can still be seen in museums around the world, including specimens in London and Dresden.

Male . . .   *. . . and female "Coco de mer" palms*

It was not until the period of French settlement in the 18th c. and the discovery of the Seychelles palm that the riddle of the coco de mer was finally solved, following which export of the nuts on a massive scale caused the market to collapse. Ruthless exploitation of the palm on the island of Praslin very quickly brought the plant to the verge of extinction. Today only about 4000 trees survive, most of them in the Vallée de Mai. They are now a protected species, subject to a rigorously enforced preservation order. The officially controlled annual harvest is restricted to 3000 nuts, the bulk of which, as in the past, are exported to India, or sold as souvenirs to tourists. Served as a dessert the jelly in the centre of the still-unripe nut is regarded as a great delicacy by the Seychellois.

The palm which bears this distinctive bipartite fruit has a 40m high, perfectly straight trunk, and very large leaves (measuring up to 16sq.m). The nut itself can weigh as much as 20kg and is by far the heaviest fruit of any kind in the world (the biggest ever found weighed 23kg and was 60cm long). The coco de mer's male seed and female fruit grow on different trees, the male palm being c. 6m taller than the female with yellow piston-like seed panicles which hang down from the dense foliage. The female trees usually produce between three and five nuts, but sometimes as many as ten.
The coco de mer grows and propagates itself very slowly – it may take as long as seven years after pollination for the nut to ripen. It is three years before germination is completed and the burgeoning shoot ceases to draw its nourishment from the nut. The female palm must be 25 years old before it can bear fruit and only attains full height after 1000 years. The age of the tallest palms in the Vallée de Mai is estimated at 800 or even 1000 years. The coco de mer has been prevented from becoming more widespread not only by its long reproductive cycle but also by the great weight of its nut. They are so heavy that they either sink immediately in water or – as with all

"Sea coconut" (Coco de mer)

those washed up on the coasts of India or Indo-China – float only because they have already dried out beforehand.

The tangled web of sexual legend which has been spun around the coco de mer's male seed and female fruit includes the myth of the supposed "mating" of the male and female palms. This is supposed to take place on stormy nights when the great leaves beat against one another. Needless to say no human being has ever witnessed this union, which is just as well because, so the story goes, anyone doing so would promptly die.

Spices were brought to the Seychelles for the first time in May 1772 by Pierre Poivre, in an attempt to break the monopoly of the spice trade enjoyed by the Dutch colony of Batavia. Later on further varieties were imported with varying degrees of success. Those still found today are vanilla – a kind of orchid, not to be confused with the native wild vanilla with its big white ephemeral flowers – the cinnamon tree, pepper, patchouli (used in the manufacture of perfume and joss-sticks), the nutmeg and the clove tree – which came from Ceylon – and also the herb lemon verbena.

Spices

Apart from decorative and useful plants there are also many poisonous ones. These become harmless when cooked and feature in the diet of the islanders. Some have an intoxicating effect and are used in nature cure remedies and medicines while others owe their poisonous reputation rather more to superstition than reality. Among the best known poisonous plants are the black nightshade, the star of Bethlehem and the strychnine tree.

Poisonous plants

Animals

The fauna of the Seychelles are one of the major attractions of a country committed to developing a "green" tourist industry, one that is "friendly"

General

to both wildlife and the environment. As with the islands' flora there are a considerable number of indigenous species, especially among the land birds. Particularly noteworthy are the giant tortoises which were once widespread across the whole archipelago. In the Mahé group today only one or two remain, the majority of those which survive being found on Aldabra Atoll where there is a colony numbering tens of thousands.

Settlement proved just as detrimental to the islands' fauna as it did to the flora. The large numbers of caymans, crocodiles and dugongs – the trusting and easily hunted sea cows with their tasty meat, found also off the north coast of Australia – which inhabited the Île aux Vaches Marines in particular (now called Bird Island), were exterminated within a few decades. It has been estimated that by 1789, barely twenty years after settlement began, 13,000 giant tortoises had already been shipped from the islands, to which must be added those made use of by the settlers themselves.

Circumstances have proved less inimicable to birdlife in the Seychelles, despite the destruction of the islands' natural bio-systems. Of the fifteen or sixteen indigenous species of land bird originally identified, thirteen have survived. In the last twenty years or so these have come to enjoy the protection of the international ornithological organisations as well as the Seychelles government. Equally noteworthy are the impressive colonies of sea birds, especially those on Bird Island where a million terns nest every year from May to October, an extraordinary – and for the visitor quite unforgettable – spectacle.

Land birds

There are 21 different species of land bird found in the Seychelles. Of these, thirteen are indigenous, the remainder having been introduced to the islands over the last 50 years. Many of the native species were decimated by predators (cats, rats, African owls) brought in by the settlers, while others suffered the loss of their natural habitats, e.g. forest or swamp. Yet more, such as the green parrot, were considered a pest and exterminated, or shot for sport as was the blue pigeon.

One of the most interesting island birds is the Seychelles paradise flycatcher (*Terpsiphone corvina*) – also called the paradise whydah – which was reduced to a few remaining individuals and for which a special reserve has now been established on La Digue. An attempt has also been made recently to re-establish it on Frégate and Praslin. The male is distinguished by its long, blue-black tail-feathers, the female having tricolor plumage (white breast, blue beak and nut-coloured wings) but no "coat-tails". It likes to nest in badamier and takamaka trees on low lying ground. The nest itself, in which a single egg is laid, is constructed from spiders' webs. Both parent birds share in looking after the chick.

Even more rare than the paradise flycatcher is the Seychelles brush warbler (*Bebrornis seychellensis*), a rather nondescript grey and green bird. It is now confined to one of the Seychelles' most interesting bird sanctuaries, Cousin Island off the coast of Praslin. Since 1968 Cousin Island has belonged to the International Council for Bird Preservation, an organisation affiliated to the World Wildlife Fund. Access is strictly controlled, being open to visitors only on certain days and then only to a limited number. Since the island became a nature reserve the number of brush warblers has increased from 26 to 300 individuals. Also found only in the Seychelles – and again only on Cousin Island – is the Seychelles warbler (*Acrocephalus seychellensis*).

Most attractive of all the endemic land birds is the blue pigeon (*Alectroenas pulcherrima*), so-called despite its multicoloured red, white and blue plumage. Being the colours of the Dutch national flag it is also known here as the "pigeon hollandais". It mainly inhabits the hills of Mahé and Frégate and the Vallée de Mai on Praslin. The related Comoro blue pigeon (*Alectroenas sganzini minor*) is found on Aldabra.

The high plateau of Frégate is also home to the last surviving magpie robins (*Copsychus seychellarum*), black birds with a slightly blue sheen and white markings on their wings. As few as nineteen are now thought to remain. One or two others are reputed to survive on Aride, Praslin, Marianne and La Digue but reports to this effect are far from consistent.

Almost as rare as the magpie robin is the white eye or Madagascar white eye (*Zosterops maderaspatana* or *Zosterops modesta*), a relative of the extinct serin (*Serina*). It is the size of a hummingbird, grey-brown in colour, and has a ring of white feathers around the eyes. With luck its far-carrying, clear warble can be heard in the hills of Mahé. Unlike the white eye, the Seychelles sunbird (*Nectarinia dussumieri*) is a true hummingbird, the smallest of the native species and owner of a powerful voice. In the nesting season the male's throat and breast turn bluey green and its axillary feathers a yellowy orange. These birds can be seen on all the larger islands as well as in Victoria.

Two endemic species of bird (albeit with European relatives which have also become established in the islands in the last few decades) are the Seychelles cave swiflet (*Collacalia francica elaphra*) and the plain brown Seychelles fody (*Foudia seychellarum*). The former belongs to the same family as our swallow, though it is dark brown with a somewhat lighter coloured breast; the latter resembles a sparrow. During the breeding season the male fody has orange patches on its breast.

Other species native to the islands are the Seychelles kestrel (*Falco aerea*), one of the world's smallest birds of prey (found on Mahé, even in Victoria), and the thick-billed bulbul (*Hypsipetes crassirostris*). The call of this dark grey bird with its light underside, orange beak, bristling head feathers and yellow legs, can be heard in the high-altitude forests on all the granite islands.

As well as indigenous species there are also some sub-species found only in the Seychelles. Among them are the moorhen (*Gallinula chloropus meridionalis* or *seychellarum*), scarcely distinguishable from its European relative, and the Seychelles turtle dove (*Streptopelia picturata rostrata*) with its ruby red head and neck. The latter is easily mistaken for the more common Madagascar turtle dove; indeed so interbred have the two become in recent times that the pure strain has all but disappeared.

The cattle egret (*Bubulcus ibis seychellarum*) is another native sub-species difficult to distinguish from its relatives elsewhere. Affectionately known to the Seychellois as "Madame Paton", the slender white bird with yellow beak and black legs is a more or less permanent resident at the market in Victoria. During the breeding season it can turn itself an attractive pink. The little egret (*Egretta garzetta dimorphia*) and grey heron (*Aredea cinerea*), members of the same family, were introduced into the Seychelles at some point in the past.

The black parrot (*Coracopsis nigra barklyi*) is the islands' only species of parrot. Its habitat is confined to the Vallée de Mai on Praslin, where it nests in the hollow trunks of dead trees close to trees bearing fruit. The striated heron (*Butorides striatus degens*), a small dark bird with a greenish back which fishes on the coral banks at low water and nests in the mangrove forests, is another bird unique to the Seychelles.

Other land birds can only be given a brief mention. The Madagascar fody (*Foudia madagascariensis*) is seen almost everywhere. In the mating season the male turns a brilliant red, either in part or from head to tail. Also

Cattle-egret – bubulcus ibis sechellarum *("Madame Paton")*

very much in evidence throughout the islands are the common mynah (*Acridotheres tristis*) and the zebra dove (*Geopelia striata*). The Arctic breeding turnstone (*Arenaria interpres*) on the other hand, is confined mainly to Cousin Island where some remain in residence throughout the year.

Sea birds

Although the Seychelles are known especially for the terns, species of gannet, frigate bird, petrel and tropic bird are also well represented.

To see the flocks of millions of sooty terns (*Sterna fuscata nubilosa*) arriving in April and May at their traditional breeding grounds in the archipelago – Bird Island in particular – is a never to be forgotten experience. They leave again in October. No one really knows exactly where these elegant black-and-grey suited aeronauts spend the rest of the year. It is even thought possible that they remain for several months on the open sea, staying entirely out of touch with land.

The white tern or herring gull (*Gygis alba monte*) with its blue beak and black eyes is one of the loveliest of the sea birds. It makes no nest, laying its single egg in an unprotected position, usually on a branch or in the open among the rocks. It inhabits virtually all the islands in the group but on Mahé was decimated when the African barn owl was introduced.

The common noddy (*Anoüs stolidus pileatus*), a rather awkward looking dark grey bird with a light grey cap, owes its name to the way it nods its head during courtship. Somewhat rarer is the lesser noddy (*Anoüs tenuirostris tenuirostris*), a slender bird with a fairly long beak. As many as 100,000 pairs breed on Aride, Cousin and Cousine during the south-east monsoon. Other members of the tern family include the swift terns (*Sterna melanauchen* and *Sterna bergi*), the South-West Pacific Island tern (*Gygis*

Sooty terns

candida), the black-naped tern (*Sterna sumatrana mathewsi*), the little tern (*Sterna albifrons*), the roseate tern (*Sterna dougallii arideensis* – most colourful of all the terns, with its bright red legs and its red and black beak) and the bridled tern (*Sterna anaethetus antartica*), a brownish coloured sub-species of the sooty tern which lives and breeds mainly on the rat-free islands of Cousin and Aride.

The gannet family is represented in the Seychelles by various types of booby, a powerful bird and an accomplished fisherman despite its ungainly body and webbed feet. Among those to be seen are the red-footed booby (*Sula sula rubripes*), the blue-faced booby (*Sula dactylatra melanops*), the abbots booby (*Sula abbotti*) and the brown booby (*Sula leucogaster*).

Largest of all the Seychelles sea birds, with a wing span of up to two metres, are the frigate birds to which Frégate Island owes its name. They can be observed from any of the granite islands in the Mahé group, but especially Aride and of course Frégate where they also breed. Their plumage is not water repellent so they cannot dive, fishing only on the surface or pirating the catch of other birds. The two best-known species are the great frigate bird (*Fregata minor*) and the lesser frigate (*Fregata ariel*).

The swift flying shearwaters, members of the petrel family, are tiny by comparison, with powerful thickset bodies, long feet and short curved beaks. The larger wedge-tailed shearwater (*Puffinus pacificus chlororhynchus*) is dark grey with black or pink feet; Audubon's shearwater has a white breast. Both nest only on rat-free islands such as Cousin and Aride. The wedge-tailed shearwater can be seen from November to March while Audubon's shearwater remains all the year round.

Last but by no means least among the sea birds are those of the Phaethontiden or tropic bird family. The white-tailed tropic bird (*Phaethon lepturus*

lepturus), the famous "paille en queue" with its two long tail feathers, is one of the most spectacular of all. It breeds throughout the year in sheltered locations on Bird, Cousin and Aride and at higher altitude on Mahé. Nests are on the ground and the young birds – silvery grey to white balls of down with black markings – are easily observed.

The red-tailed tropic bird (*Phaethon rubricauda rubricauda*), somewhat larger than the "paille de queue", is the rarest of the sea birds which nest in the Seychelles. It is found on Aride, Aldabra and Cosmoledo.

Other land animals

Reptiles

Like crocodiles, giant tortoises (*Testuda gigantea*) are relics of the saurian age. This unique species was virtually exterminated on many islands in the Seychelles by the early settlers who ruthlessly exploited the trade in its much sought-after meat. Only on Aldabra is there now a colony of any size, between 150,000 and 180,000 individuals. They weigh more than 50kg and usually live for 60 to 70 years – though they can grow to 400kg in weight, 1.50m in length, a metre in height, and have a life span of as much as 150 years. The largest and oldest known giant tortoise is "Esmeralda" on Bird Island. The only other species of tortoise on the islands is the African black terrapin (*Pelusius subniger*) found on La Digue and to a lesser extent Cousin.

Crocodiles and caymans were exterminated very early in the islands' history. The only reptiles remaining apart from giant tortoises are various kinds of skinks and geckos, two sorts of adders (*Boodon geometricus* and *Lycognathopi seychellensis*), the black blind-snake (*Typhlops braminus*), and the chameleon (*Cameleo tigris*).

Geckos are everywhere. The most commonly seen are the little white and grey geckos (*Phelsuma astriata*) on Mahé and the bright green variety on La

Giant tortoise

Gecko

Digue – welcome house-guests since they keep down the mosquitoes and other insects.

Skinks on the other hand inhabit the rat-free islands which support sea bird colonies. Among the varieties are the lidless skink (*Ablepharus boutonii*), the scelotes skink (*Scelotes braueri*) and two sorts of mabuyas (*Mabuy seychellensis* and *Mabuy wrightii*).

The insects of the Seychelles are actually of more interest than the reptiles, 65% of the relatively small selection of *c.* 300 species being unique to the islands. This by itself is proof that the separation of the islands from the continents of Asia and Africa occurred far back in the earth's history.

Insects

The only mammal indigenous to the Seychelles is the flying fox (*Pteropus seychellensis*). This large bat can be seen at night in woods and on the beaches. It can easily be mistaken in the dark for a large bird.

Mammals ("flying fox")

Underwater Life

The marine life of the Seychelles is as beautiful and as fascinating as anywhere on earth. Some 300 types of fish and more than 100 species of coral make up an underwater world of great diversity and delightful colours, a world which to a large extent can be explored simply snorkelling in shallow water.

General

The submarine landscapes of the coral islands differ markedly from those of the Mahé group, where granite outcrops dominate as they do on the islands themselves. Though lacking the fantastic variety of shapes found in the coral jungles of the Red Sea, the Maldives or Australia's Great Barrier Reef, the Seychelles are particularly noted for the richness of their fishlife.

31

It was in the Seychelles that Jacques Yves Cousteau, the well-known French marine scientist and producer of documentary films, made his famous film "The Silent World" (1955).

N.B.   See the Practical Information section at the end of this guide for details regarding sea-angling and big-game fishing, diving and snorkelling and suggestions on where to dive off some of the islands.

Fish

The wealth of fish in the waters encircling the Seychelles is little short of incredible. Big-game fishermen know this best of all, many a record having been broken here. But there is plenty of scope for those content just to observe the myriads of colourful fish in all their wonderful variety. Emperor angel fish (*Pomacanthus imperator*), black-barred triggerfish (*Rhinecanthus aculeatus*), shrimpfish (*Aeoliscus strigatus*) and tigerfish (*Pterois radiata*) share their territory with parrotfish (*Scarus sp.*), smooth dogfish (*Triaenodon obesus*), moray eels (*Muraenidae*), butterfly fish (*Cheatodontidae*), myripristis (*Myripristis adustus*) and the strange mudhopper (*Periphthalmus*) which breathes air and can spend lengthy periods out of the water on the sand or rocks.

Sharks – about eighteen different varieties including the much feared white shark, the hammerhead, the man-eater, the tiger and the blue shark – are met with beyond the reefs which shelter the lagoons. In addition there are also barracuda, mackerel, sea bream, herring, sardine, flying fish, spear fish and a great variety of tuna.

The stonefish or devilfish (*Synanceia verrucosa*) is so good at camouflaging itself that it becomes completely invisible against its coral or stony background. It is exceedingly dangerous to humans who tread on its very long and very sharp spines, so stout shoes or plimsoles with thick rubber

Fire fish (pterois radiata)

Parrot-fish (scarus sp.)

soles should always be worn when walking in shallow water or on coral banks exposed by the tide. Anyone treading on a stonefish should get medical attention immediately.

Corals and coral banks

Contrary to first appearances corals are not plants but colonies of small animals called polyps. The bizarre, colourful and often flower- or fern-like fabric of the reef, which lends an almost psychedelic quality to exploring the submarine world of the tropical oceans, is entirely made up of their limy skeletons of calcium carbonate.

Corals

For their growth corals need a combination of sunlight, warm clear water, and a plentiful supply of food (mainly plankton and minute shellfish). In the Seychelles this means they thrive mainly on the south-east side of the islands, where a strong, steady flow of fresh warm seawater produces an ideal habitat.

Except for one or two species capable of withstanding exposure for short periods at low water, living coral must remain submerged. Coral larvae usually settle on the skeletons of dead corals, contributing little by little to the reef-building which, over centuries, results in the growth of enormous coral banks. These can extend for as much as 4000m from the seabed to the surface.

Coral banks (reefs) consist primarily of the skeletons of dead corals, but also of the limy deposits left by many other marine creatures (such as molluscs, worms, algae and sponges). One major constituent of coral reefs is halimeda, a type of algae which acts as a sort of cement for the coral. Some kinds of coral attach themselves to rocks. These then become the base of a fringing reef, skirting a rocky island or growing up around the rim

Coral banks

Red spigot-coral

of a submerged volcanic crater – the process by which atolls are formed.
Only a few corals can establish themselves on sand.

The coral's sole natural enemy is the crown-of-thorns starfish. Although its
spines are not equipped with barbs like those of the sea urchin, and so are
less painful to humans, it clamps its stomach over the coral's limy shell and
sucks out the polyp. This predatory creature is capable of causing large
scale devastation, quickly transforming whole reefs into barren moon-
scapes (as has happened in Australia). Fortunately in the Seychelles they
have not appeared in such threatening numbers.

Shellfish and snails

There are 320 kinds of shellfish and snails found in the Seychelles, of which
the various types of cowrie are the best known and most beautiful (*Cypraea
mappa, Cypraea lamarcki, Cypraea walkeri, Cypraea tigris, Cypraea mone-
ta, Cypraea annulus*). Some species of cone shell and marine trumpet are
also brightly patterned, their colours and shapes blending in natural harmony. The most familiar of these, the trumpet shell (*Charonia tritonis*), is
now a protected species, being the one creature to prey on the coral-eating
crown-of-thorns starfish. The exceptionally pretty cone shell Geographicus
should be treated with extreme caution; the poison exuded by its small
spines can prove fatal. Cone shells of any kind found on the beach or in
shallow water should never be touched with bare hands. Wear gloves for
protection when handling them and always transport them in some form of
solid container.

Helmets (*Cassides*), Turbinidae (*Turbo argurostromus*), augur shells (*Tere-
brides*), Vasidae (*Vasum turbinellus*), spiny thorn oysters (*Spondylides*)
and mother-of-pearl trimmed Preoceres are among the many other species
which abound in the Seychelles, contributing to the islands' colourful
variety.

Turtles

Turtles have for centuries been hunted for their tortoise-shell – long ago the ancient Egyptians fashioned everyday objects such as combs from it. In the early days of colonialism large quantities were exported from the Seychelles to Mauritius, Réunion and India. So swiftly did stocks threaten to decline that quotas limiting catches were introduced as early as 1800. Even so, at the beginning of this century some 10,000 turtles were still being slaughtered every year on Aldabra Island.

Loveliest of all and hence most highly prized is the translucent shell of the hawksbill turtle (*Eretmochelys imbricata*), fully grown at three years old and up to a metre in length. The loggerhead turtle (*Caretta caretta*) is somewhat larger and can weigh as much as 350kg. The biggest turtle is the leatherback (*Dermochelys coracea*), measuring up to 2m and weighing 600kg.

Green turtles (*Chelonia mydas*) are much sought after for their meat, used to make green turtle soup. The females come ashore every three years on the beaches of the coral islands, arriving at nightfall to lay their eggs in holes hollowed out with their flippers and then carefully filled in again. (Arrangements can sometimes be made to observe the egg laying. Anyone watching should keep quiet and well out of sight; otherwise the turtles are disturbed and flee back into the ocean.) The young turtles emerge after about ten weeks and must scrabble their way down the beach to the sea and the safety of deep water as swiftly as they can. Most in fact fall prey to birds and crabs in the course of this short but perilous journey.

Turtles today are a protected species and the import of tortoise-shell into Europe is strictly prohibited. Any temptation to buy items of tortoise-shell on sale at the markets on Mahé and Praslin should be resisted. Not only do such souvenirs face confiscation by Customs on arrival in Europe but, by not buying, tourists can genuinely help to protect these gentle creatures.

Hawksbill turtles

Protected species

The Country and its People

The Seychelles is now a republic, its official name (in the country's three languages of English, French and Creole) being the Republic of Seychelles, République des Seychelles or Repiblik Sesel. It is a one-party state, the only political party allowed being the "Seychelles People's Progressive Front" (SPPF). The 25 representatives who make up the single-chamber parliament (National Assembly) enjoy only limited legislative power. The office of President of the Republic – held at present by France Albert René – combines that of Head of State, First Secretary of the SPPF and Commander-in-Chief of the armed forces. The president is nominated by the SPPF, standing for election at a general election which no opposition candidate can contest.

The Seychelles are divided into 24 administrative areas and constituencies called "districts". Twenty of these are on Mahé, two on Praslin and one on La Digue.

The islands' government is responsible for carrying out SPPF decisions. Under the president's direct control are six state secretariats (planning and external affairs, finance, justice, defence, tourism, and aviation), as well as the "Presidential Office". The president appoints seven ministers whose portfolios cover internal affairs, political organisations, transport, education and information, health, employment and social security, and national development.

Since the 1977 coup which brought President France Albert René to power the Seychelles has had its own army and militia. These were greatly

Political system

Official crest

Government

*Seychelles
national flag*

35

strengthened following the unsuccessful putsch by South African mercenaries in 1981. Regular forces now number about 1200 men (army 83.4%, navy 8.3%, and airforce 8.3%), in addition to which there is a paramilitary militia trained by the army. Military expenditure now totals c. 5.6% of GNP (gross national product; world average 5.9%).

Population

The Republic of Seychelles has a population of 67,000, of whom 88.5% live on the island of Mahé and its immediate satellites. Praslin and neighbouring islands have 4650 inhabitants (7.5%), La Digue 2000 (3%), Silhouette 250, and the remainder of the Mahé group a total of 150. In all only 660 people (1%) live on the Amirantes and the outlying islands. Some 37.2% of the population is urban, the remaining 62.8% of Seychellois being country dwellers. Average population density is 145.6/sq.km, though on Mahé it is 400/sq.km and on Praslin and La Digue 100 and 150/sq.km respectively.

For some years vastly inflated predictions were made of likely population growth (the result of employing inappropriate statistical models). Thus a decade ago the population of the islands at the end of the 1980s was projected to be 85,000. The actual growth rate – i.e. births (1700 to 1800, c. 2.5% as opposed to 2.9% in 1980) less deaths (500, c. 0.76%, world average 0.99%) and loss by emigration – amounted to an increase of only some 300 a year. The fact is that, every year, between 500 and 1000 people (1 to 1.5% of the population) leave the country. Australia (15,000), Great Britain, East Africa and Canada all have significant Seychellois minorities.

The greater part (over 89%) of the population is of African descent, having ancestors who were either slaves brought over in the 18th or 19th c. by the settlers or by pirates, or who were quite literally unloaded from slave ships onto the islands by the British navy following the abolition of the slave trade. Since then however so much intermarriage has taken place with Europeans and Asians that a completely distinct people has emerged. The rest of the Seychelles population is made up of Chinese (1.6%), Indians (4.7%) and Europeans. The Chinese, comparative newcomers to the islands in the last few decades, have been quick to integrate with the rest of the population. Indians, on the other hand, tend to marry almost exclusively within their own community.

Social problems

Although the society of the Seychelles is thoroughly multi-racial, lightskinned Seychellois nevertheless enjoy a certain superiority of status. This is reflected particularly in the choice of marriage partners approved by, if not actually made by, parents for their offspring. A phenomenon peculiar to the Seychelles is the enormously high rate (73%) of illegitimate births, largely the result of tight restrictions on divorce imposed by the Catholic Church to which the vast majority of Seychellois belong. Also, in the seventies and eighties one child in four was born to a mother under 18 years of age, by far the highest such rate in the world.

Almost 40% of the population of the Seychelles are under 15 years of age, nearly 68% below 30. Infant mortality (babies under a year) is 1.84%, lower than in some marginal areas of Europe. Average life expectancy is 71 years (66.2 for men and 73.5 for women).

About 43% of the population (27,000) have regular or seasonal work, 20,000 being in permanent employment. Wages are very low by European standards.

An initial building boom followed the opening of the islands' international airport in 1971, coming to an abrupt halt in 1973. Periods of quite high unemployment dogged the seventies and eighties. Since then the demand for both skilled and unskilled labour has increased to such an extent that

Seychellois in Market Street, Victoria ▶

the government is considering bringing some foreign workers into the country.

In the wake of the social changes of the seventies and eighties alcohol consumption rose considerably. Some statistics put the per capita consumption of alcohol in the Seychelles as the fourth highest in the world.

Health service

Thanks to considerable efforts made over the last decade the Seychelles now have a health service which, by Third World standards, is excellent – doctors, dentists, mental health and skilled medical workers (about one skilled medical worker per 1000 inhabitants), as well as nurses and ancillary staff. There are 350 hospital beds in all, about 250 of which are in Victoria. Almost every settlement has its own small clinic. Severely ill patients are taken by ambulance or air to the main hospital in Victoria (see also Practical Information, Medical Assistance).

Folk medicine

The older Seychellois in particular still possess a good knowledge of traditional remedies and the numerous plants with curative properties – estimated to be between 250 and 500. The practice of traditional medicine however is closely associated with various forms of superstition and witchcraft. Though deeply rooted in the Seychelles these are officially banned and so this type of medicine is not encouraged.

Religion

There is no official religion in the Seychelles. More than 90% of the population are Catholic, 8% are Anglican, and the rest belong to a variety of religious denominations. Many forms of superstition, magic and mysticism are still prevalent, despite being banned as long ago as 1958 by the then colonial government. The beliefs and practices of the male and female witchdoctors, soothsayers and faith-healers ("bonhommes di bois" and "bonfemmes di bois") are not unlike to those of the West African voodoo cult, making similar use of amulets ("gris-gris"), various powders, dolls and magic signs.

Despite these similarities the ethnologist Burton Benedict who has spent many years studying the society of the Seychelles suggests that the beliefs and practices which survive today probably owe more to European than to African tradition. He argues that the separation of the slaves from their culture roots was so total that no system of tribal religion could possibly have translated itself and survived in the following centuries. African rituals for example are so closely bound up with the socio-economic framework of tribal life (e.g. with cycles of growth and fertility) that they would at once lose all raison d'être and significance. This would have been particularly true in the case of the slaves, passive victims on whom an entirely alien colonial culture was summarily imposed.
Benedict points rather to similarities with European traditions of superstition and witchcraft, arguing that such beliefs are likely to have been imported into the islands by Europeans just as the more "orthodox" Catholicism was. The fact of the matter seems to be that the mystical beliefs and practices of the European and African traditions have so much in common that it would be difficult to distinguish precisely between them.

Economy

General

Being a small country with a limited economic base, the Republic of the Seychelles suffers from many of the economic ills afflicting the Third World. In common with other islands in the Indian and Pacific Oceans, as well as the countries around their shores, the Seychelles began by looking to tourism for an initial cure.
During the early periods of French and then British colonial rule, the chief commodities exported were precious woods and, later, tortoises. Reckless exploitation of these natural resources quickly brought an end to this source of income.

Coconuts, and the copra that comes from them, then took over as the staple of the islands' economy. In the early years of this century cinnamon (particularly oil of cinnamon produced from the leaves) came to equal copra in importance, and this remained the position until the 1970s when tourism replaced them as the major industry and foreign currency earner.

In recent years a rather more traditional Seychellois activity, fishing, has also seen something of a transformation. Over a relatively short period of time systematic modernisation and the introduction of factory processing have seen the industry develop into one of the mainstays of the islands' economy. Fish-processing is in fact far more advantageous to the Seychelles' balance of trade than tourism (which actually increases dependence on imported goods in a country already short of foreign currency).

The contribution made by individual sectors of the economy to the gross national product of *c.* US$260 million a year is as follows: agriculture 6%, industry and construction 14%, tourism and related activities 11%, transport and retailing 27%, services and other 42%. Of the 20,000 in permanent employment some 8,000 work in the service sector, 2,300 in agriculture and fishing, and 2,500 in hotels and catering. GNP per capita of the population is US$3800 (compare Portugal US$3670).

In the years immediately following the granting of independence in 1976 priority was given to social improvements (in education, health and housing). From the late seventies onwards however the emphasis shifted to the industrial sector. Additionally, after an initial period in which a policy of speedy and widespread nationalisation was implemented, private investment is once again being actively sought and encouraged, especially in the form of joint ventures with foreign participation.

Agriculture and fishing

Because in the early years of settlement an abundance of natural resources existed "for the picking", and because when these were exhausted a good income could be secured from coconut plantations which were simple and inexpensive to run, agriculture in the Seychelles remained relatively undeveloped. In recent years, with the construction of the new airport and the boom in hotel building which followed, agricultural land, always scarce, has been in even shorter supply. At the same time the presence of large numbers of tourists increased the islands' dependence on foodstuffs from abroad. Food imports doubled between 1970 and 1975 and doubled again by 1979. Most of the basic necessities such as beef, milk, fruit, vegetables, flour and sugar are now brought in from South Africa.

About 25.9% of land in the Seychelles is used for agriculture, 18.5% for forestry. In recent decades the islands have ceased to be self-sufficient in all food products apart from fish and coconuts. Some indication of the grave crisis in the agricultural sector is the continuing exodus of workers from the land, beginning in the 1960s and intensifying in the 1970s.

European vegetables tend not to thrive in the Seychelles. Among the vegetables which do grow well are manioc, potatoes, sweet corn, tomatoes, cabbages, green salad, yams, avocados, pumpkins, sweet potatoes and aubergines. These are mainly cultivated by private growers. Tea and coffee have been produced for a number of years now on plantations at intermediate altitudes in the Mahé hills, and there is a profusion of fruit almost everywhere. Virtually every known variety of tropical fruit has been introduced into the Seychelles over the last 200 years – various kinds of mango ("Blanc", "Fisette", "Périse", "Malabar", "Kinon", etc.), the breadfruit tree with its beautiful blooms and green fruit, the cashew tree, papayas, pineapples, lychees, citrus fruits, the atherhoas tree with its

Food crops

refreshing fruit which can be eaten on its own or in a salad, and finally seventeen or so varieties of bananas (of which the best known are "Malgache", "Noire", "Figre", "Gros Michel", "Monsieur", "Mile", "Cendre", "Rouge", "Gabou" and "Saint Jacques", the latter growing up to 60cm in length.

Some years ago two large model farms were established on Mahé's west coast in an attempt to tackle the problem of agricultural underdevelopment. As well as contributing their own production to the country's total output they are also used to demonstrate new crops and methods of cultivation. Current developments include a number of flower (orchid) growing projects, regarded as a promising new source of foreign exchange.

Copra

From the 1830s and 1840s, after the freeing of the slaves, labour was less easy to come by and labour costs rose. At the same time demand for coco-products increased on the world market and the coconut and its derivatives became the islands' main export crop. While at the beginning of the century coconut groves were mainly found only along a narrow coastal strip, the subsequent spread of plantations was such that they soon covered all the islands' cultivatable land. Even today there are still c. 10,000 hectares under coconut palms, a little less than a fifth of the total area.

Until about 1900 the main coco-product was coconut oil, of which several hundred thousand litres was already being exported annually by 1840. At the start of the 20th c. the export of coconut oil was replaced by copra, the dried and ground kernel of the nut, containing 66% fat, 20% carbohydrate and 8% protein. This is processed further into coconut oil, used in the manufacture of glycerine, synthetic resins, cooking oil, candles, soap and shampoo. Seychelles copra is among the best in the world and for a long time constituted the country's major source of income. By the mid-1980s exports had fallen dramatically however (2374 tonnes of copra were exported in 1986, only 130 tonnes in 1987).

Cinnamon

The cinnamon tree was one of the earliest spice plants introduced into the Seychelles, the first seeds having been brought to Mahé by Pierre Poivre as early as 1772. It was not until the 1920s however, when vanilla production was badly affected by a combination of disease and a price collapse on the world market, that the potential of cinnamon was developed to the full. The bark is stripped from the trees and oven dried, before being ground or distilled, together with the leaves, to make oil of cinnamon (eugenol), used in the manufacture of vanilla. In recent years the lowering of raw material prices worldwide has made it increasingly difficult to find an outlet for the islands' cinnamon. The volume of cinnamon products exported from the Seychelles fell from 1600 tonnes in 1973 to a mere 300 tonnes in 1980.

Fishing

The annual per capita consumption of fish in the Seychelles (in excess of 80kg) is the highest in the world. Up to now fishing by the islanders has been on a relatively limited scale, generally family ventures using some 400 mainly small craft. Commercial exploitation of the wealth of fish in the surrounding waters has been left to the fishing fleets of other nations. However, since establishing the internationally recognised 320km Exclusive Economic Zone extending over a total area of about 1 million sq.km, the Seychelles have been able to introduce fees for the granting of licences to fish. This has gone some way towards reducing the foreign trade deficit as well as financing the development of the islands' fish-processing industry and providing resources for the construction of their own fishing fleet. This latter possibility has been under active consideration for a number of years.

At present the international fishing fleet on permanent station around the islands consists of 50 craft, including 40 large vessels from EC countries (in particular France and Spain). As well as the permanent fleet there are about 100 other craft belonging to such fishing nations as Japan and the Soviet Union.

Fisherman at work (La Digue)

Recently two vessels were leased from France, intended to form the nucleus of a fishing fleet of their own. However, they were quickly found to be unsuitable, the Seychellois being unable to handle them. The islands' new national development plan now has provision for the construction of two craft, financed by the European Development Bank.

Catches taken from Seychelles waters consist almost entirely of tuna. So as not to endanger stocks special nets are used which allow fish below a certain size to escape.

The islands' first fish cannery began operating in Victoria in the middle of 1987. Its output of 10,000 tonnes results from the processing of 20,000 tonnes of raw fish. A second plant now under construction should increase total production to some 40,000 tonnes. The income generated by the export of tinned tuna has lifted the total export earnings of the Republic of the Seychelles from 15 to 35 million rupees. This is a welcome counterbalance to the decline in exports of cinnamon and copra.

In a related project on the island of Coëtivy the Island Development Company is establishing a crab farm with a planned annual output of 800 tonnes. Waste fish-meal from the tuna cannery will provide feed.

Industry and foreign trade

Seychelles industry is still in the early stages of development. During the period of British colonial rule no attempt was made to establish any "home-grown" industry, and in the 1970s priority was given to exploiting the potential of tourism. Since the early 1980s however, a modest degree of industrialisation has been part of the country's economic development plan. In addition to the fish-cannery already referred to, the islands now

41

have a reasonably well-established construction industry and a modest involvement in shipbuilding, timber products, brewing, brush manufacture, synthetics, metal and leather processing, detergents and tobacco. Guano and granite are the only industrial raw materials found locally. Supplies of guano – the droppings of sea birds accumulated over centuries especially on the coral islands and used as fertiliser – are slowly running out on many islands. Since 1840 more than 1 million tonnes has been collected from the island of Assomption alone, most of it going to Mauritius.

In 1986 66.5 million kw of electricity were generated; by 1989 this had increased to 94.3 million kw. An adequate public power supply is maintained on all the larger islands. On the smaller granite islands and on the coral islands power comes from private generators.

Foreign trade

Chief among the exports of the Seychelles are canned fish, copra, fish, cinnamon, oil of cinnamon, coconuts, guano, vanilla and tea. Following the coup which brought France Albert René to power, control over trade was vested in the Seychelles Marketing Board. Now however there is a move towards greater liberalisation as a means of encouraging economic activity. As far as imports are concerned the islands' main trading partners are Great Britain, France, South Africa, Yemen, Singapore and Japan; exports go primarily to France, Pakistan and Réunion.

Postage stamps are a further important source of foreign currency for the islands, being eagerly sought after by collectors all over the world. Their contribution to the balance of trade has already overtaken that of copra and cinnamon.

Even so the Republic of Seychelles has acute problems with its balance of payments, being heavily in deficit. Food and drink, tobacco and mineral oils are the country's main imports.

Postage stamps, an important article for export

Tourism and transport

Since the early 1970s tourism has burgeoned into one of the country's major industries. In the year before the tuna cannery opened tourism provided 70% of foreign earnings. Today it still accounts for more than a third of GNP, making the Seychelles one of the leading tourist nations of the world in terms of its contribution to the overall economy.

Tourism

Before the airport was built the journey to the Seychelles by sea took 42 days and there were correspondingly few visitors. From the moment Pointe La Rue Airport was opened in 1971 the number increased rapidly: 15,000 visited the islands in 1972 and in 1978 tourists exceeded islanders for the first time. While in 1959 there were only five hotels and a guest house, between 1970 and 1980 the number of tourist beds rose from 140 to 2600. In the late 1970s expectations were high, an increase to 125,000 visitors being anticipated in the next decade. These expectations however remained unfulfilled. In 1982 and 1983 the tourist industry suffered a severe set-back owing to the political instability in the country.

Today though more than 100,000 visitors – mainly from France, Italy, Great Britain, Switzerland and Germany – come to the Seychelles every year in search of the sun. While the proportion of visitors from Europe has risen steadily, the number of South Africans holidaying in the islands has tended to fall in recent years.

The islands can now provide more than 3600 tourist beds, with an occupancy rate of between 65 and 70%. Of these 85% are on Mahé, the principal island. A further 800 to 900 beds are planned, but beyond that no more visitor accommodation is projected since government policy is to keep tourism within manageable bounds. The reason given for this farsighted decision is the need to protect the sensitive eco-systems of the islands and their waters. Instead of further expansion priority is to be given to improving and modernising transport on and between the islands, the telephone network, and accommodation on the outer islands. At the same time it is intended to renovate those of Mahé's hotels which are already outmoded and to bring facilities up to present day standards.

Mahé's international airport was opened in 1971. Today it handles over 1650 international flights a year, as well as 6000 flights between the islands. In the late 1980s passengers travelling on international flights averaged

Transport

Stamps with the emblem of the World Wildlife Fund

about 78,000 annually (plus 86,000 in transit). Passengers on internal flights totalled some 140,000 of whom 83,000 were foreign visitors.

Apart from Mahé the islands which have either an airport or a landing strip are: Praslin, Frégate, Bird, Desroches, Denis, Darros, Marie Louise, Rémire, Alphonse, Astove, Farquhar and Coëtivy.

Almost 80% of the country's 269km of roads (of which 165km are tarred) are on Mahé (i.e. 203km, 141km tarred). There are some 50km (19km tarred) on Praslin and 16km (5km tarred) on La Digue. Although there are only a few thousand cars, lorries and buses to use them, small jams can still build up at peak times on the main roads in and out of Victoria.

History

The earliest Persian and Arab seafarers, familiar with the Persian Gulf and probably the coast of Africa, almost certainly knew of the existence of the Seychelles. Documentary proof however is lacking; there is no mention of the islands, even in the "Périple de la mer d'Erythrée", the first ever sailing directions for the Indian Ocean written in the 1st c. B.C.

From 1000 B.C.

The island of Madagascar is settled by people from Malaya who are presumed to have used the Seychelles as a staging post on their journey. The existence of casuarina trees on the islands suppport to this assumption – the likelihood of the seeds being carried naturally across the vast ocean distances is small.

200 B.C.

Arab seafarers and traders visit the Seychelles, which appear for the first time on Arab charts drawn up in the 9th c. There is also a reference to "tall islands" on the sea route to the Maldives in 14th c. manuscripts written by two Arab merchants Al Mas'eudi and Ibn Battutta. Thirty or so old graves discovered in the Anse Lascars on Silhouette in 1910 are probably those of crew from an Arab trading vessel. The name "Aldabra", from the Arabic "al khadra" meaning "the green one", also suggests an Arab presence in the islands. In 14th and 15th c. Arabic texts the Seychelles are found referred to as "zarin" ("the sisters").

A.D. 700–1000

At about this time the Portuguese navigator João de Nova discovers the islands of the Farquhar group and the Seychelles are shown for the first time on Portuguese charts (by Alberto Cantino dated 1502). From 1506 onwards they frequently appear under the name "as sete irmas" ("the seven sisters"; on a map by Pedro Reinel) or "os irmãos" ("the brothers"). The principal island is usually called "Y. Rana".

1501 (or 1502)

On his second voyage to India Vasco da Gama discovers the islands of the Amirantes group. The Portuguese quest for alternative routes to the spice islands of the East Indies ushers in the Age of Discovery.
Unlike the Portuguese the Dutch, equally intent on securing a position for themselves in the Far East, show little interest in the Seychelles and other islands en route. The only Dutch settlement appears to have been on one of the smaller, more isolated islands between 1598 and 1712.

1502 (or 1503)

On 19th January two ships of an East India Company expedition (Fourth Voyage of the East India Company), anchor off Mahé. "Ascension" and "Good Hope" are commanded by Alexander Sharpeigh whose commission is to establish trade relations with countries bordering the Indian Ocean. Landings are made on Ste Anne, North, Silhouette and Praslin, all of which appear uninhabited.

1609

From 1685 onwards piracy is regularly reported in the area, a major threat to British seafarers in particular. This follows the determined action taken against pirates in the West Indies. The Indian Ocean becomes the periodic haunt of buccaneers such as Read, Williams, Avery, White, Bowen, Howard and Captain Kidd as well as the Frenchmen Misson and Olivier Levasseur (called "La Buse", the Buzzard). Their piratical reign lasts for almost 50 years. La Buse and Taylor (an Englishman nicknamed "the Terror of India") make frequent marauding expeditions. Among their prizes are the "Vierge du Cap" carrying perhaps the biggest haul of loot in the history of piracy, and two richly laden merchantmen belonging to the Companie des Indes, the "Duchesse de Noailles" and "Ville d'Ostende". This provokes the French authorities to take action, apprehending La Buse in 1730 and executing him on the Île Bourbon (now Réunion). Tradition has it that La Buse's

From 1685

legendary treasure lies hidden somewhere at the western end of Beau Vallon Bay on Mahé. A number of expensive searches have been mounted but so far without success.

1742   On 22nd November Captain Lazare Picault anchors his two vessels the "Elisabeth" and "Le Charlie" in a bay on the south-west coast of Mahé, christening the island "Île d'Abondance" ("Isle of Abundance"). The expedition, organised by the Governor of the French Île de France (Mauritius) Bertrand François Mahé de Labourdonnais, leaves the island after four days having taken 300 giant tortoises and 600 coconuts on board.

1744   Because the spoils of Picault's first expedition are so meagre and his survey incomplete, Labourdonnais sends him on a second voyage of exploration to the islands. This time Picault lands on 30th May at a spot close to present day Victoria. He renames the island "Mahé" in honour of the Governor and christens the archipelago as a whole the "Îles de Labourdonnais". During a two-year campaign in India which he leads in person Labourdonnais becomes the victim of colonial rivalry and intrigue. Returning to the Île de France (Mauritius) he finds a new Governor installed. Finally he is executed in the Bastille.

1756   On 9th November the Irish sea captain Corneille Nicolas Morphey (in command of "Le Cerf" and "St Benoit") lays official claim to Mahé and the seven islands to the east of it on behalf of Louis XV of France. A "pierre de possession" is erected, forestalling British intentions to establish a colony. The island group is named after Jean Moreau de Séchelles, Louis XV's Minister of Finance from 1754 to 1756.

1768   The ships "La Digue" and "Curieuse" under the command of Marion Dufresne sail to the Seychelles on an expedition commissioned by the French Minister of Marine Gabriel de Choiseul, Duke of Praslin. Duchemin, captain of the "Curieuse", lands on the Île aux Palmes which is renamed "Praslin" in honour of the expedition's patron. A stone of possession is again erected laying official claim to the island, as Morphey had done on Mahé. It is in the course of this expedition that a surveyor called Barré solves the "mystery" of the legendary coco de mer.

1769   Duchemin undertakes a second voyage to Praslin, loading his ship "L'Heureuse Marie" with cocos de mer for sale in India. But he seriously miscalculates the profits to be made. By flooding the market and dispelling the aura of mystery surrounding the hitherto legendary coco de mer (by revealing that the nut is after all quite commonplace origin), he causes the price to collapse.

1770   On 27th August fourteen French settlers and a small group of seven African slaves are landed on the island of Ste Anne in Victoria Bay to establish the first long-term settlement in the Seychelles. The driving force behind the settlement, though never setting foot on the Seychelles himself, is Brayer de Barré, a former official receiver of the Lotterie de l'Ecole Royale Militaire at Rouen. His ship the "Télémaque", commanded by Captain Lecorce, leaves the Île de France (Mauritius) on 12th August, arriving at Ste Anne fifteen days later. Despite express instructions to develop the islands agriculturally the settlers have only one objective, to amass as large a fortune as possible in the shortest possible time. As a result they concentrate their efforts on exploiting the islands' natural wealth, in particular the timber and giant tortoises.

1771   Pierre Poivre dispatches Antoine Gillot to Mahé with a 40-strong workforce plus a group of slaves. His instructions are to find a suitable site on which to establish spice gardens – the "Jardin du Roi"; the location he selects is Anse Royal. Friction soon develops however between the new settlers and those on Ste Anne, so that in 1778 the Governor of the Île de France arranges for a contingent of fifteen soldiers to be stationed permanently on the island. Their camp, at first called "l'Établissement" and then, unofficially, "Port Royal", is the nucleus from which the present-day capital Victoria later evolves. A British expedition consisting of the ships "Drake" and "Eagle" visits the islands of the Mahé, Bird and Amirantes groups.

Pierre Poivre introduces cinnamon trees into the Seychelles. In the same year a certain M. Hangard arrives on Ste Anne, the first French settler not to return to France or Mauritius on completion of a fixed-term contract. 1772

In May a vessel believed to be a British frigate appears in Victoria Bay. Following strict orders the officer commanding the small garrison, de Romainville by name, immediately sets fire to the spice plantations of the "Jardin du Roi" to prevent them falling into British hands. It soon transpires however that the ship is actually sailing under the French flag, which fact had been concealed for fear of encountering the British. 1780

The resident population of the islands has grown to several hundred; they include fourteen slaves in Établissement, eleven whites, 232 slaves and a free black and his son on Rest-Mahé, and a white settler with thirteen slaves on Praslin. Jean Baptiste Philogene de Malavois, Governor of the Seychelles, initiates the first attempt at systematic development. Every free settler is allocated land with a requirement that he cultivate it. An ultimately unsuccessful attempt is also made to halt the over-exploitation of the islands' animal population and precious woods. 1785

Malavois introduces a number of laws which even today still form the basis of legal practice in the Seychelles. 1786/87

After the outbreak of the French Revolution France agrees to the Seychelles becoming a base for pirates amd privateers who, with as many as 200 ships, are preying on British merchantmen plying the Indian Ocean trade routes. Robert Surcouf, self-styled "King of the Corsairs", is reputed to have attacked and looted 40 vessels. 1789

The free settlers decide to set up an elected Colonial Assembly, one of the first acts of which is to declare their independence from other French colonies. But Seychellois enthusiasm for the Revolution wanes the following year when the French National Assembly abolishes slavery. 1790

The Chevalier Quéau de Quinssy is appointed Governor, bringing with him the – for the settlers – "good" news that the ban on keeping slaves has been lifted again. He sets up the islands' shipbuilding industry (the largest ship launched from Mahé's yards is the "Thomas Blyth" (1820), a merchant vessel of 335 tonnes) and establishes a number of plantations.
This same year sees the first attack on the Seychelles by the British navy. On 16th May four ships under the command of Commodore Newcombe appear off Victoria armed with a total of 166 cannon and carrying 1200 soldiers. Faced with such overwhelming odds de Quinssy has no option but to surrender. The following morning he signs an Act of Capitulation, drawn up largely by himself, which in effect guarantees that the status quo will be maintained on the islands. Over the years to 1811 de Quinssy is forced to capitulate to the British seven times, on each occasion hoisting the French flag again as soon as they have sailed away. 1794

The colony now has 591 inhabitants, of whom 487 are slaves. 1798

The harbour at Établissement is the scene of bloody engagements between two British warships which appear unexpectedly and two French ships which have brought exiled Jacobin revolutionaries to the islands. One of the French vessels is captured, the other sunk. 1801

De Quinssy capitulates for the last time to the British, who annexe the islands. The 1814 Treaty of Paris (ratified in 1815 by the Congress of Vienna) 1811 confirms British sovereignty over the Seychelles. De Quinssy, by now held in high esteem by the British, is invited to stay on in the service of the King. This he does, changing his name to de Quincey. Until his death in 1827 he continues to act as mediator between the British administration and the French settlers.

1812   The British government declares the slave trade illegal and Governor Sullivan frees any slaves brought to the island by traders. It is only in the 1830s however that the trade is finally quashed; so dependent are the settlers on slave labour that illegal trading goes on for years. It is estimated that the number of slaves shipped to the Mascarene Islands and the Seychelles between 1670 and 1810 totals about 160,000 (of whom 45% are from Madagascar, 40% from East Africa, 13% from India and 2% from West Africa). Virtually without exception, throughout this period between 85 and 90% of the islands' inhabitants are slaves.

1818   The Seychelles now have a population of 5690. In the following year an observer notes that Mahé and Praslin and also La Digue and Silhouette have been stripped of most of their natural forest vegetation.

1833   The Abolition Act making slavery illegal is passed by the British Parliament, leading eventually in 1839 to the emancipation of slaves in the Seychelles. Even then the islands become an involuntary home for many ex-slaves released from slave ships by the British navy and brought here instead of returning to their native lands. Documents from 1861 preserved in the National Museum at Victoria prove also that some trade in human beings continues after emancipation. Since 6000 of the islands' 7500 inhabitants are ex-slaves, many of whom understandably refuse to work for their former masters, agriculture on the islands is in crisis. In contrast to Mauritius where some 450,000 Indian workers are brought in between 1835 and 1907, settlers in the Seychelles receive no similar assistance from the British government. The crisis is made all the worse because, starting in the 1820s, cotton, at that time the islands' main export crop, faces increasing competition from America. In a short space of time the price of cotton on the world market falls by two thirds. Many planters emigrate to Mauritius where sugar-cane plantations promise a better living. Between 1830 and 1840 the population of the Seychelles shrinks from 8500 to 4360. Prompted by the growing world trade in coconut oil and copra the emphasis of the islands' economy shifts to coconut plantations (with copra mills) which can be run without the need for large numbers of workers.

1840   The economy and population of the Seychelles reach something of a nadir with only 4360 now living on the islands. The following year the Seychellois decide to mark the Queen's marriage by changing the name of Établissement to Victoria.

1851   The first Catholic diocese is established in Victoria.

1862   On 12th October a hurricane strikes Mahé causing a landslide which destroys the town and large tracts of coconut plantation. In a single night a hundred people lose their lives.

1869   The opening of the Suez Canal on 17th November brings great benefits to the Seychelles, which now lie on the new and very much shorter shipping route to Asia. Exports are considerably facilitated. The main export commodities at this time are coconuts and vanilla.

1875   Sultan Abdullah Khan of Perak and his retinue are the first of a long series of deportees exiled to the Seychelles. In the 88 years up to 1963 they are followed by King Prempeh of the Ashanti and his household, seventeen chiefs and two kings from the Gold Coast, the Kabaka of Buganda and the King of Bunyoro (now both part of Uganda), three members of the Amer-

ican Watchtower Bible and Tract Society of Nyasaland, Mahomed Ali Shir-
rey, a Sultan from Somaliland, Seyid Khalid bin Bargash, heir to the
Sultanate of Zanzibar, Saad Zaghul Pascha of Egypt and four members of
his cabinet, Ali bin Ahmed Fadh and five henchmen from Aden, Hussein
Fehri Effendi al Khalidi and four other Palestinians, Archbishop Makarios
and three supporters from Cyprus, and Afri Didi from the Maldives.

The population of the islands reaches 14,191 but is soon to be drastically **1881**
reduced by small-pox epidemics in 1887 and 1895.

Cables linking the Seychelles to Zanzibar and Mauritius bring tele- **1893**
communications to the islands. The first hospital is built on Mahé.

On 31st August the Seychelles cease to be Mauritian dependencies. The **1903**
Mahé group and the coral islands apart from Coëtivy and Farquhar amalga-
mate to form a British Crown Colony in their own right.

Coëtivy's links with Mauritius are also severed and the island joins the **1908**
Seychelles.

The First World War has the effect of isolating the Seychelles once again **1914**
from the rest of the world, plunging the islands' economy into yet another
severe crisis. Poverty becomes widespread and with it crime – for a time
2500 out of a population of 24,000 are in custody. In 1919 the economic
situation recovers, only to collapse afresh around 1929. Their heavy
dependence on exports condemns the islands to a period of chronic economic instability until the end of the Second World War.

Electricity comes to Victoria. **1923**

Farquhar also passes from Mauritius to the Seychelles. **1932**

The official currency becomes the Seychelles rupee. **1934**

For the first time the inhabitants of the Seychelles are granted a limited **1948**
degree of suffrage. About 2000 persons become eligible to vote, entitle-
ment depending on literacy and ownership of land. The legislative council
is made up of twelve members, four of whom are elected. With enfran-
chisement so restricted the "Seychelles Taxpayer's and Producer's Association" wins all four elected seats in each election held up to 1963.

The first two political parties, the Seychelles Democratic Party (SDP) and **1964**
the Seychelles People's United Party (SPUP) are formed. In the 1970s the
SDP campaigns for full integration with the United Kingdom; the SPUP on
the other hand pursues the goal of independence from the start. In 1970
elections are held for a ruling council which is to have some influence over
decisions taken by the Governor. The SDP receives 53.8% of the votes, the
SPUP 44.2%.

Universal adult suffrage is introduced. In a referendum the Seychellois **1967**
vote in favour of maintaining the ties with Great Britain. In the elections the
SDP wins four of the eight elected seats in the legislative council, the SPUP
three (the remaining deputy is an Independent).

The first constitutional conference is held. The Seychelles are granted limited **1970**
autonomy while retaining the status of a Crown Colony for the time being.
Many Seychellois believe the islands would have little chance of prosper-
ing if forced to "go it alone". Britain however is committed to a policy of
decolonisation, influenced by considerations of national and international
politics. James R. Mancham becomes the islands' Chief Minister and then
Prime Minister.

The international airport is opened. Air Kenya has already inaugurated the **1971**
first air service from Mombasa the previous year.

History

1972	The new deep water port is constructed.
1973	The SPUP is recognised as an official liberation movement by the OAU (Organisation of African Unity).
1974	Fresh elections give the SDP 52.4% of the vote and the SPUP 47.4%. Under the British electoral system however the SDP win thirteen seats in the House of Deputies, the SPUP only three. The two parties form a coalition government.
1976	On 26th June the Seychelles become an independent republic with James R. Mancham (SDP) as the first President. He forms a coalition government with France Albert René's SPUP. The Republic's internal policy is at first geared to a market economy and its foreign policy pro-Western.
1977	On 5th June, while James R. Mancham is abroad representing the Republic of Seychelles at the Commonwealth Conference in London, his Prime Minister France Albert René (of the Seychelles People's Progressive Front/ SPPF; Front Progressiste du Peuple Seychellois/FPPS) seizes power in a coup. Tanzania provides military support.
1979	René's position as President is confirmed in a general election in which he is unopposed. Thereafter Seychelles politics take on a moderate socialist orientation. An initial phase of compulsory nationalisation and an attempt at creating a centrally planned economy is followed in the 1980s by a more liberal approach.
1981	An attempted putsch by South African mercenaries masquerading as a visiting rugby team fails when their weapons are discovered by an airport customs official. After a shoot-out the rebels escape in a hijacked airliner.
1984	President René is elected for a second term of office.
1986	Pope John Paul II visits the Seychelles.
1987	The country celebrates the tenth anniversary of its "liberation" when France Albert René seized power.
1989	Having fallen drastically for a while in the early 1980s the number of visitors to the Seychelles recovers to exceed 100,000 for the first time. In the mid-year presidential elections René is once again confirmed as President, his third period in office.
1990	Although there is some criticism of President René for his failure to liberalise the country, his one-party State appears to be in no danger.
N.B.	The Seychelles are the chosen venue for the 1993 Indian Ocean Games.

Famous People

Listed alphabetically below are well-known people who were born, lived or died in the Seychelles or who have played a prominent role in the islands' history.

N.B.

Vasco da Gama, reputed to have been a man of great courage but quick temper, was born in Sines, a port in southern Portugal. Under the patronage of King Manuel I he set sail from Rastello near Lisbon on 8th July 1497 in search of a sea route to India. He had with him four ships and a crew of 170 men, together with a number of priests and convicts. Having passed the Canary Islands a week after departure, the ships rounded the Cape of Good Hope on 22nd November and sailed north up the east coast of Africa before eventually striking eastwards and arriving off the west coast of Hindustan in May 1498. They set out on the return voyage on 8th October, reaching Lisbon again on 10th July 1499. Although da Gama came back almost empty handed from this expedition, wherever his exploits became known there was admiration and envy for the man who had braved the unknown to reach the fabled spice islands. He was lavishly rewarded by the King who also bestowed on him the title of "Dom".

Vasco da Gama (c. 1460 to 24.12.1524)

In 1502/03 da Gama embarked on his second voyage to India, this time at the head of a large fleet. It was on this journey that, on passage up the Indian Ocean in 1502 or 1503, he discovered – not far off the coast of East Africa – the "Ilhas do Almirante" ("Admiral Islands"; today called the "Amirantes"), a cluster of coral islands which extend south-eastwards from Mahé and the granite islands in the Seychelles group, and which have now been part of the Seychelles for more than 90 years.

Da Gama left on his third and final voyage to India in 1524, having been appointed Portuguese viceroy by the King. He died on 24th December 1524, only four months after his arrival. The great navigator's achievements are celebrated in "The Lusiads" by the Portuguese writer Luis Vaz de Camões (1524/25–1580).

Hodoul was one of the most notorious of the French corsairs whose activities made the Indian Ocean unsafe for merchant vessels towards the end of the 18th c. Born in Ciotat in southern France he cleverly took advantage of the struggle between France and Britain for regional supremacy to cloak his activities in a mantle of semi-legality. He captured a large number of British and Portuguese merchant ships, some of which carried very valuable cargoes. Although the Seychelles officially became British territory in 1794 they always offered Hodoul a refuge from the British navy's ever increasing threat. In fact, after losing his ship to the British, he was able to pass his twilight years on Mahé, taking up permanent residence there and becoming a magistrate under the British administration. Hodoul Island, a small island in Victoria harbour, is named after him.

Jean François Hodoul (d. 5.1.1835)

Olivier Levasseur was perhaps the most infamous of all the French pirates who sailed the waters of the Indian Ocean. Like the Britons Taylor and Edward England, Levasseur (or "the Terror of the Indian Ocean" as he also came to be known) arrived on the scene in the early years of the 18th c. This was after the pirates' favourite "hunting ground", the West Indian Antilles, had become too unsafe for their comfort, the British authorities having decided to put an end to their constant harassment by using the full force of the navy against them. In July 1720 "La Buse" appeared in the Comoros Islands, where he teamed up with Taylor, a former British naval officer. Between them they gathered together 500 men and for a number of years terrorised merchant shipping in the area. As long as they only attacked British, Portuguese and Dutch vessels they enjoyed the sympathy of the

Olivier Levasseur, called "La Buse" ("The Buzzard") (d. 7.7.1730)

Famous People

Vasco da Gama

James R. Mancham

France Albert René

French settlers and authorities. But in 1721 "La Buse" made the mistake of attacking the "Duchesse de Noailles", a ship belonging to the Compagnie des Indes. For this the French never forgave him, even though he is said to have given back part of the spoils. Between 1721 and 1724 Levasseur and about 250 men probably operated from a base near what is now the little settlement of Bel Ombre on the Seychelles island of Mahé. Remains of the camp and pirate graves can still be seen there. (Repeated attempts have also been made to locate Levasseur's treasure, reputed to be worth more than 500 million US$ and said to be buried on the island.) In 1730, after being shipwrecked in a storm, "La Buse" was arrested on Madagascar by the French authorities of the "Île Bourbon" (now the island of Réunion). Offered his freedom in return for his vast treasure he refused and was hanged in Saint-Paul (until 1738 the capital of Mauritius) on 7th July 1730, apparently throwing into the crowd beforehand a clue to the whereabouts of his loot.

James R.
Mancham
(b. 1939)

James R. Mancham, son of one of Mahé's wealthiest traders, studied law in London and worked as a barrister there in the early 1960s. In 1963 he returned to the Seychelles, founding the Seychelles Democratic Party (SDP) and a newspaper ("Seychelles Weekly"). In 1964 at the age of 25 he was elected a member of the ruling council and in 1970 became the islands' first Chief Minister under British colonial rule. In due course he became Prime Minister and, after independence (in 1976), the first President of the Republic of Seychelles. Mancham, something of a playboy by reputation, planned to turn the islands into a tropical paradise for the world's jet set. Assiduous cultivation of contacts, private as well as diplomatic, meant constant travelling abroad. It was while he was away on one of these trips that he was removed from power by his Prime Minister, France Albert René.

Lazare Picault
(c. 1700 to
21.2.1748)

Lazare Picault was a seafarer born in Toulon in about 1700. He rose to take overall command of ships of the Compagnie des Indes operating in the waters around the Île de France (now Mauritius) and the Île Bourbon (now Réunion). In 1742 he was commissioned by the Governor of the Île de France, Bertrand François Mahé de Labourdonnais, to explore the area to the north of the French colony and to seek a shorter sea route from the Mascarenes (the archipelago to which Réunion and Mauritius belong) to India. On 19th December 1742 he came across some islands which he at first took to be the "Three Brothers" ("Trois Frères"), only to realise on his way back that he had made a mistake and that the islands must have been a distinct and hitherto unknown group. In 1744 he was sent off again by Mahé de Labourdonnais to confirm his discovery. This time Picault took possession of one of the islands for France, renaming it Mahé, and rechristened the whole group of islands the "Îles de Labourdonnais".

Poivre, son of a merchant, was born in Lyons in 1719 and studied at mission schools in Lyons and Paris. He joined the Order of St Joseph and was sent to China. In Canton he was wrongly imprisoned and in order to defend himself learned Chinese. On his way back to France his ship was intercepted by the British, and in the ensuing battle he lost his right arm. He was put ashore in Batavia (since 1950, Jakarta, capital of Indonesia), where he learned about spice growing over which at that time the Dutch had a total monopoly. In 1746 he arrived on the Île de France as a member of Mahé de Labourdonnais's entourage. Back in France again Poivre found himself barred from the priesthood on account of his missing limb. He joined the Compagnie des Indes, proposing to found a settlement in Cochin-China (the Mekong River lowlands in southern Vietnam) with the intention of breaking the Dutch monopoly of the spice trade. Between 1749 and 1754 he undertook two expeditions from the Île de France to Manila, bringing back with him a large number of spices which however were later through carelessness destroyed. Poivre is then believed to have returned to France in 1756, settling once more in the Lyons area to devote himself to his studies. In 1766 however he received a royal summons to take over the post of "Intendant", joint head of administration in the Île de France. In the course of three further expeditions he was then able to obtain the much prized spice seeds. In addition Poivre introduced printing to the island, laid out the famous botanic garden in the grounds of Labourdonnais's former residence Pamplemousses, and helped give the colony new financial impetus. He had Port Louis (capital of Mauritius) and its harbour rebuilt and attracted a number of scientists and explorers to the island. In 1772 he organised the successful introduction of spice plants into the Seychelles. Setting off for home for the last time that same year, he eventually died in Hyères on the Côte d'Azur in 1786.

Pierre Poivre
(23.8.1719 to
6.1.1786)

Prempeh, King of the Ashanti tribe from West Africa, was deported to the Seychelles by the colonial authorities in 1900 after surrendering to a British peace-keeping force. His entire household – his mother, three of his wives and 55 attendants, joined the following year by 21 more Ashanti chiefs with their wives, families and entourages – accompanied him into exile. Prempeh held court in the Seychelles just as if it were his homeland, though he was eventually to renounce polygamy and be baptised. He was allowed to return home in 1924.
Prempeh was followed by a whole series of other prominent exiles – King Unvanga of Buganda, John Bunjoro from Uganda, Sultan Mahmud Ali from Somaliland, and the Egyptian Prime Minister Saas Zaghloul Pascha together with five fellow Egyptian politicians. Some, like Archbishop Makarios, even seem to have enjoyed their banishment. In 1947 Amin al Huseini, the Grand Mufti of Jerusalem who was opposed to the division of Palestine into separate Jewish and Arab states, became yet another exile to the islands. A 1952 plan of Churchill's to deport 5000 Irish nationalists to the Seychelles was never carried out however.

King Prempeh
(c. 1872 to
1934/35)

Quéau de Quinssy was born in Paris, the son of a groom. He embarked on a military career, and from 1775 to 1779 was a lieutenant in the service of Louis XVI's brother. This took him first to India, but towards the end of 1779 he arrived on the Île de France (later to be Mauritius). In 1791 he was dispatched to Paris to attend a meeting of the National Assembly, where he made representations on behalf of troops stationed on the Île de France against their low wages. In 1793 he was appointed Military Commandant of the Seychelles, arriving on 9th September of that year aboard the "Aimée". He took a great personal interest in the development of agriculture and cattle rearing, and introduced bee keeping, silk worm cultivation and tortoise breeding. During his administration the population of the islands grew continuously. From 16th May 1794 onwards he was forced to capitulate to the British navy and the superior fire-power of its ships on no fewer than seven occasions, but no sooner had they sailed away again than the French tricolor was broken out once more. When the British finally took

Jean-Baptiste
Quéau de Quinssy
(1751 to 10.7.1827)

possession of the islands, Quéau de Quinssy continued in various official capacities, first as Commandant and then as a magistrate. In 1816 he was suspended by the new Commandant, Edward Madge, for alleged abuse of office, but in 1817, following his acquittal by a naval court in London, was reinstated. He remained a magistrate on Mahé until his death in 1827.

France Albert
René
(b. 16.11.1935)

France Albert René was born in 1935, the son of a plantation manager on the island of Farquhar. In the early fifties he attended a Swiss seminary before studying law in London. In 1958 he went back to the Seychelles for three years, returning to complete his studies at the London School of Economics from 1961 to 1964. In England he was an active member of the Labour Party. In 1973 his Seychelles People's United Party (SPUP) was granted recognition as a national liberation movement in the Seychelles by the Organisation of African Unity (OAU) and in the 1974 elections received over 47% of the votes. Under the British electoral system however, the party won only three of the sixteen elected seats in the colonial Assembly. When James R. Mancham became the first President of the newly independent Republic of Seychelles in 1976, he appointed René his Prime Minister. But on 5th June 1977, with the aid of Tanzania, René mounted a coup against Mancham, taking over the reins of power himself. In 1979 René – the sole candidate – was elected the new president of the Republic of Seychelles, since when his position has been twice confirmed in the elections of 1984 and 1989.

A scene on a Seychelles island, painted by Michael Adams ▶

Art and Culture

Although the period of French rule was relatively short compared to the two hundred years of British sovereignty which followed, it is nevertheless French cultural influences which are most evident in the Seychelles, as also in Mauritius. Whereas these Indian Ocean colonies were peopled over two centuries mainly by French settlers and African slaves, the British presence was frequently little more than an administrative one, a handful of officials and a small garrison. Furthermore, contrary to widely held belief, most traces of African culture disappeared fairly rapidly. The uprooting of the slaves left any cultural inheritance severed from its socio-economic context, depriving traditional religions, beliefs and customs of their continuing relevance.

Language

The official languages of the Seychelles are English, French and, since 1st August 1981, Creole. Creole is the mother tongue of 95% of the population. About half also speak English, and some 37% French. A further 0.5% are Gujarati speaking Indians, 0.4% Chinese and 1.5% speak other languages. When Creole was made an official language it also became the language of instruction in junior schools (having previously been banned from the classroom throughout the colonial period). Since then most prime time television and radio programmes are broadcast in Creole as well.
Creole – or "Kreol" as it is called by linguists seeking to establish it as the authentic literary language of the Creole-speaking Indian Ocean island nations – is a patois originating 90% from old colonial French (the "vieux français bourbon"). Over the centuries it has evolved its own grammar, pronunciation and syntax while at the same time incorporating elements of English (3.5% of the vocabulary) and Madagascan (1%). Beginning in the early 1960s the grammar of this language (which until then had lacked a written form) became the focus of increasingly intense study. The "Kreol Institute" in Mont Fleuri (a suburb of Victoria) is dedicated to such research.

Seychelles Creole is noticeably different from that spoken by other ethnic groups in the Indian Ocean (Réunion, Mauritius, Rodrigues), and even more so from the Creole spoken in the Caribbean. All have many features in common however, and have a shared origin in a form of proto-Creole. Speakers of the different dialects are able to understand one another.
Although Creole is the mother tongue of the Seychellois and as such is used for most purposes, it is an odd fact that they seem to prefer English when discussing matters close to their hearts.

Education

Under British colonial rule the Seychelles were without any form of public education until as recently as 1947. Prior to that the only schools were mission schools, helped by no more than a modest amount of government grant-in-aid. In 1947 however the then Governor, P. Selwyn-Clarke – after whom Victoria's market is named – brought some private schools under state control, a step condemned by Mahé's wealthier inhabitants as "socialism".
Nowadays education is compulsory for every child from the age of four. There are schools on all four of the main islands, Mahé, Praslin, La Digue and Silhouette, and c. 95% of children of school age attend classes. Some 14,500 children are enrolled in Seychelles primary schools and there are a further 4000 secondary pupils (together representing almost a third of the population). With barely 1200 teachers to service all levels of education about 1400 students are at teacher-training college. Even today 14% of the population have never been to school and only 57% of Seychellois over the age of fifteen (55% of men, 60% of women) can read and write. To tackle the problem of adult illiteracy a comprehensive programme of further education has been started in recent years.

In addition to two levels of compulsory education the system includes a third optional level. The two pre-school years and nine years of schooling proper can be followed by two years National Youth Service (NYS). Although officially voluntary in practice National Youth Service is a pre-requisite for embarking on any further education in the Seychelles and, more especially, for receiving any grant for study abroad. These grants can be given for the study of virtually any subject in any country, but awards are based on criteria of national economic need. In fact only about half the islands' young people go on to National Youth Service after leaving school. Many families choose instead to send their school-leavers abroad straight away at their own expense. Youngsters who do spend their two years in the National Youth Service camps are not permitted to spend a single night at home in all that time, being allowed to visit their families only twice a month (for twelve hours). Their education in the NYS camps includes some para-military training, carried out primarily in the Port Launay area in the north-west corner of Mahé.

During their early years at school children are taught in Creole. They start learning English at seven and French a year later.

Creole literature is still very much in its infancy, the one or two writers and poets who lived in the Seychelles in colonial times having almost all written in French. The first novel to be written in Creole was "Mon Tann En Leokri" by Antoine Abel (b. 27.11.1934). It appeared in 1982.

The founding of the "Creole Institute" in 1990 was the first of a series of measures intended to nurture literary talent in the Seychelles e.g. by means of competitions for novels in Creole. Already there is a small group of younger writers who are gaining recognition for their work, especially their poetry.

Literature

It is only in the last fifteen years or so that painting in its more familiar forms has made an appearance in the Seychelles, a development for which the artist Michael Adams has been mainly responsible. Adams, born the son of a planter in Malaysia in 1937, grew up in Tanzania and Cornwall (England). At the age of fifteen he began studying art in London, later working there as an engraver at the Royal College of Art. Returning to Africa he took a post as an art teacher in the Ugandan capital Kampala before settling in Kenya in the mid-1960s to work as a freelance artist. Since 1972 he has been living in the Anse aux Poules Bleues in south Mahé. His extremely attractive paintings have earned him the reputation of "the 20th c. Gauguin", vividly capturing the atmosphere of the Seychelles. His favourite media are water-colours, silk and screen printing and etching.

Art and craftwork

Of the younger generation of artists the best known are Donald Adelaide, Serge Rouillin and Léon Radegonde. A good overall perspective on the work of artists in the Seychelles and the style of their painting – the most obvious parallels are with primitivism – can be gained in the little galleries in Victoria and on visits to the artists' studios themselves (see Practical Information, Museums and Galleries, Souvenirs).

Craftwork, like painting, is an activity which has made its appearance only relatively recently in the islands. Generally speaking only the simplest everyday objects tended to be made in colonial times, seldom of much interest from an aesthetic point of view. With the growth of tourism however arts and crafts received a new kind of stimulus in the 1970s. As a result Indonesian-style batik, woodworking (using various precious woods) and model making (ship models in particular) are very much in evidence today.

The most primitive form of music and dance (and one in which African influence can still to some extent be discerned) is the "moutia", a musical rendering of the prayers and rituals of the early slaves. The dance is usually performed in the open air to an accompaniment of large tambourin-like drums made from kid or the cured skin of the giant ray, warmed over a fire to increase the resonance. The dancers face one another without contact,

Music and dance

the steps consisting of a sidewards skipping shuffle with a simultaneous rotation of the hips and upper part of the body.

Nowadays the Seychelles version of the Mauritian "séga" is more likely to be seen than the "moutia", danced here – unlike in Mauritius – to an accompaniment of tom-toms. In recent years commercialisation and the advent of Western pop music have seen even more radical stylistic innovations superimposed on what nevertheless remains a traditional dance (still performed with all its resonances of Africa on the Mauritian island of Rodrigues for example).

Finally there is the "contredanse", originally English but adopted by the French in the 18th c. First introduced at the court of Louis XIV from where it eventually spread to the colonies, it is a combination of waltz, polka and allemande danced to the music of a Camtole (Kamtolé) band.

The Seychelles in Quotations

". . . we found many coconuts of various kinds, already ripe and green, birds and tortoises (but our men would not eat them, even though we could have killed the tortoises with our sticks) and many rays and other fish. And in addition there were many crocodiles in the fresh-water rivers. Our men caught one of the crocodiles alive, tied a rope round its neck and pulled it ashore. On one of these islands, less than two miles from where we had landed, we later found one of the best timbers which I have ever seen. The tree is tall and thick and the wood really hard. There are many trees which have no branches below 20 to 25 metres; they are thick and straight as an arrow. This is a very good place to rest and refresh oneself, with the fine timber, the water, coconuts, fish and birds, and no danger apart from the crocodiles."

John Jourdain
(journalist 17th c.)

(John Jourdain, a British journalist, was on board one of the ships under the command of Alexander Sharpeigh which reached the Seychelles in 1609)

"On this day, armed as always, we landed but found nobody and no evidence that anyone had been here before. We called it L'Isle d'Abondance. On the shore there were many coconut palms bearing fruit, and tortoises and turtles, but not many. There was drinking water in abundance and trees which were ideal as masts for all kinds of ships, especially when repairs were necessary. . . . It is a pity that this island does not lie between 15° and 20° on the route to India, for settlements could be established here. The place seems good to us; it often rains, especially in the hills. the Evening dew is very heavy and the island has fish in abundance."

Lazare Picault
(mariner 1742)

". . . the next day we discovered a fine harbour in the reef of the island, which is surrounded on the eastern side by seven other islands. On the 9th of the same month we sailed into this harbour and at once began to explore the entire island, the coasts, the interior and the mountains. The various valuable trees which grow everywhere on the island astonished us as did the harbour, of which we made a plan. Here 50 large warships could find shelter; in addition there is room for careening and repairing every kind of vessel. Considering these advantages and firmly convinced that the island can be useful to the state, we had a boulder set up on a high rock at the entrance to the harbour, with the arms of France chiselled in it. We also set up a mast on which at sunrise today the royal standard was raised."

Nicolas Morphey
(captain of a
frigate)
November 1756

"The climate and the soil of the Seychelles, lying in latitude 4°54' south of the equator, are very favourable and provide good yields. There are many turtles, turtle doves, ringed doves, blue doves, parakeets, bats, tortoises, reticulated tortoises on the neighbouring islands and in the archipelago. Wild animals of all kinds, hordes of wild goats, seabirds, fish in abundance, dugongs, timber for shipbuilding, rosewood, wood for joinery and for making masts. Nearly all the islands of the archipelago are thickly wooded, all have tortoises as well as fresh-water and game. The situation of the harbour, which has several through channels, is pleasant and secure. . . Since its foundation six years ago the settlement has experienced no hurricanes. It is extremely important to protect the harbour so that one can find refuge here."

Brayer du Barré
1775

"This archipelago consists of a pile of granite cliffs on which chalk has been superimposed. Seen from a distance they provide a fine spectacle, since many of them are covered with trees; the ground is, however, rough, stony and full of ravines and steep hills. On the other hand they have a pleasant climate and do not suffer from the storms to which the islands in the south

Gottlieb August
Wimmer

are exposed. The larger islands have a few streams and springs, and considering their considerable distance from the mainland there is a very striking fact concerning the geographical distribution of animals – here there is a species of crocodile which grows up to five feet in length. There are many fishes and turtles near the coasts. The forests are notable for the beautiful plumage of the birds. Pineapples, cucumbers, peppers and tomatoes grow wild. The maledive or sea coconut is very agreeable."
("Latest pictures from Africa and its islands" 1834)

Suggested Routes and Walks

Preliminary note

Apart from Mahé and Praslin all the islands are small enough to be explored quickly and easily on foot or, in the case of La Digue, bicycle. The suggestions below only refer therefore to the two larger islands; they include three drives on Mahé (the principal island) and a number of walks on Mahé and Praslin.

Distances (shown in brackets after the route headings) are rounded to the nearest kilometre.

Suggested routes

N.B.

It will be found helpful to refer to the map provided when planning any of these excursions.

1. A drive around the northern tip of Mahé (20km)

This circular tour of the northern part of the island, the shortest of the three routes, can easily be completed in half a day. Leave Victoria via Albert Street and Castor Road (or alternatively go past the harbour and along 5th June Avenue) driving north through the suburbs of English River, Union Vale and Pointe Conan. On reaching Anse Étoile (about 4km from Victoria, beyond De Quincey village) a detour on the La Gogue road leads to the centre of the peninsula (see Walks; Mahé: no. 1).

Continuing north along the coast road from De Quincey village, stop for a moment at La Retraite; the little boatyard there is full of interest. The next port of call is Anse Nord D'Est with its very long beach. Here a German called Pit Hugelmann distils a highly distinctive perfume from local plant extracts. He generally keeps open house for visitors.

Once past the pretty little Charana Beach and the settlement of Machabée at the island's northern end, both coast and road turn south, with villas strung along the hillside to the left. The tiny secluded bays with good bathing make delightful spots at which to pause and rest. A tropical garden and a fine view of North Island are among the pleasant surprises in store for visitors to Glacis, one of the seaside communities here.

Mahé's principal tourist area extends southward from Glacis, around the shores of Beau Vallon Bay. Here lovely batiks will be found for sale in Ron Gerlach's boutique (at the near end of Beau Vallon's very long beach). There are boat trips from Beau Vallon to Silhouette, Thérèse and Conception as well as along the highly scenic north-west coast of Mahé itself.

The road continues west of Beau Vallon, passing more beach hotels and (opposite Fisherman's Cove Hotel) the hotel catering school where visitors can sample the culinary skills of a new generation of Seychellois cooks. Some of the islands' best restaurants are found on this stretch of road, justly known therefore as the "Gourmet Mile".
A short detour inland leads to Bel Ombre where the church has a much revered statue of St Rochus. The saint reputedly intervened to halt a small-pox epidemic in 1884.

At Danzilles where the motor road comes to an end clear traces of excavations can be seen (on the right). These were carried out only a few years ago

Machabée at the northern tip of Mahé

as part of a search for the legendary treasure of the pirate La Buse, the "Terror of the Indian Ocean" (see Famous People: Olivier Levasseur). There is also a walk from here to Anse Major where there is excellent diving and snorkelling (see Walks; Mahé: no. 2).

Returning to Beau Vallon follow the road to Victoria as it ascends to the St Louis Pass. At the top a road goes off to the right to Le Niol, a mountain village from where there are beautiful views over Beau Vallon Bay and across to the island of Silhouette. A short distance along the Le Niol road there is a turn-off on the left to Bel Air, a suburb of Victoria. Bel Air's narrow streets lead into Sans Souci Road in Victoria itself.
The main road however zigzags down through the densely populated suburb of St Louis with its colourful houses, past a fine colonial house (now the Marie Antoinette Restaurant) which stands above the road on the left, and finally via the perfectly straight Revolution Avenue back to the heart of the capital.

2. A drive round the south of Mahé (48km)

The clock tower in Victoria's Albert Street also makes a good starting point for the longest and perhaps most interesting of the three drives on Mahé. This time however head south along Francis Rachel Street, past the mosque tucked away to the right, past the modern colonial style headquarters of Cable and Wireless, past the park in which stands the new National Library, then into Mont Fleuri Road and on in the direction of the airport.

Just beyond the junction with Liberation Avenue is a cul-de-sac which leads to the Botanic Garden, and the cemetery (on the right immediately past the intersection of Mont Fleuri Road and Belvedere Road) provides a magnificent view of the harbour and the islands of the Ste Anne group. About 500m further on the premises of a car rental company also house the studio of the artist G. Devoud. His eye-catching pictures in bold colours vividly capture the landscape and people of the Seychelles.

Souvenir-hunters are welcome too at the Seychelles Pottery in Mamelles, a suburb of Victoria about 4km south of the city centre. Lying on the shore here and also worth a visit is the "Île de Farquhar", an old sailing ship. Forming an impressive backdrop to the local clinic is a fine example of the kind of rock formation typical of Mahé. These distinctive "glacis", with their unusually pronounced and regular erosion channels, dominate the coastal scenery.

Leaving Mamelles continue south, first passing a small lagoon dotted with huge granite "marbles", and then the Seychelles brewery, open to the public on weekdays. Now mangrove swamps border the road on its sea-ward side and visible beyond are the 124ha of reclaimed land by which Mahé has been enlarged – the result partly of the fringing reef sanding up following the building of the airport and partly of deliberate reclamation. Next come three small settlements (or more accurately, colourful jumbles of corrugated iron huts) called Zig Zag, Le Rocher and Petit Paris, behind which tower granite masses culminating in impressive peaks. At Cascade, another small community c. 6km from Victoria, there is a typical Seychelles church and a walk which follows the course of the little Rivière Cascade up to a waterfall. Anyone with time for a stroll will also see the local women at work, doing their day's washing in the mouth of the stream. For a while beyond Cascade the road is flanked by "open" water, a lagoon on one side and mangrove swamps on the other. This stretch is not without its hazards as some of the boarding at the edge of the road is missing.

Anonyme Island, in view beyond the airport runway on the left, apparently still has some giant tortoises living in the wild. Soon the last of the indus-trial complexes which punctuate the scene at intervals between here and Victoria is left behind and the palm plantation landscape of South Mahé beckons ahead.

2 or 3km south of Pointe La Rue the road drops down to a bay called Anse aux Pins. Into sight on the left, after a sharp bend, comes the "Katiolo" discothèque. This is where the island's young people gather, particularly at weekends. The nearby Reef Hotel has a golf-course which the road skirts for a while on the right-hand side.

A short distance before the turn-off for Montagne Posée, the "Maison St Joseph" comes into view. Following its restoration this former colonial residence is now used by the Ministry of Education. It was the setting for some of the scenes in one of the "Emanuelle" films. All sorts of elaborate souvenirs are manufactured in the recently opened Creole Craft Village – anything from model ships, tinware and woodworking to embroideries, needlework and beach clothes. In a palm grove directly behind the Village is a cinnamon and copra factory which can be visited on request. A few hundred metres further on there is another opportunity to watch model ships being made, at "La Marine".

Beyond Pointe au Sel (from where there is a lovely view of Anse Royale bay) the Mahé landscape becomes flatter. The scrubland between the road and the beach here is a popular evening trysting place for the island's courting couples. The first of the beaches at the northern end of Anse Royale is also one of the favourite bathing places in South Mahé. There is excellent diving and snorkelling in the shelter of the coral reef which fringes this part of the coast for almost its entire length.

From Anse Royale the road continues past Anse Bougainville (starting point for a walk across the island through the plantations of the Val d'Endor estate) towards the southern tip of Mahé, once a part of the island much frequented by holidaymakers. Nowadays however it is definitely not a place to visit – the two most southerly bays are used for military mano-euvres, often involving a great deal of shooting. Shortly after Anse Forbans (another pirate haunt in days gone by), the road turns inland and climbs for 2km or so to Quatre Bornes. From here a detour can be made via the Grand Police road to Anse Intendance, scenically one of Mahé's loveliest spots. Also very attractive is the remote Anse Bazarca where – being unprotected by any fringing reef – massive ocean breakers pound the coast with scarcely a pause. They make a wonderful spectacle but bathing is forbidden because of the dangerous currents.

From Quatre Bornes the drive follows the main road as it heads for Mahé's south-west coast and Anse Takamaka, at the north end of which are the spectacular "granite slides". These drop down from the road to the water, to be buffeted by the ocean swell.

Next, having skirted Anse Gaulettes, we reach Baie Lazare, from where a splendid walk which starts at the Val Mer Estate (Hotel Plantation Club) goes over to Pointe Lazare (see Walks; Mahé: no. 8).
The road itself continues to Baie Lazare village where, not far beyond the police station, a small, partly surfaced but generally very poor and bumpy track leads to two more bays, Anse Soleil and Anse la Liberté.

1 or 2km beyond Baie Lazare village the artist Michael Adam's house comes into view on the left, surrounded by tropical vegetation. There is a small permanent exhibition of his work. Afterwards the route follows the curve of Anse à la Mouche, past the turn-off to Les Cannelles and the Sancta Maria coconut plantation, past a number of excellent restaurants (worth keeping in mind by those planning to dine out in the evenings), and on to Anse Boileau. A little further on the Montagne Posée road branches off eastwards away from the coast and climbs into the hills (there is no signpost but the turn-off is easy enough to spot, being the only one to head inland after Anse Boileau). It ascends from the valley of the Jouanis river to the top of the Bon Espoir Pass, the site since 1976 of the Seychelles Cable and Wireless Corporation's overseas transmitting station. On either side of the road, hidden away in the thick vegetation, are a number of elegant villas. A superb vista opens of the Anse aux Pins below, before the road descends again, twisting and turning, to the island's east coast, rejoining the coastal road to the international airport and Victoria.

3. A drive through the highlands and along Mahé's west coast (30km)

Start once again at the clock tower and drive south along Francis Rachel Street. Just before the Botanic Garden turn right into Liberation Road, which soon winds its way uphill to the junction with Sans Souci Road. At each of the various bends and also at the junction there are fine views over Victoria, the harbour, and the islands of the Ste Anne group. More elbows and curves follow as the road makes its way through the suburbs of Bel Air and Sans Souci and past the villa in which Archbishop Makarios lived during his exile in the 1950s (now the American embassy). A little beyond it is a sign indicating the start of the footpath to the "Trois Frères" peak (see Walks; Mahé: no. 3).

Two traffic barriers, military vehicles, and sentries guarding a gate at the highest point of the road (called Forêt Noire Road) indicate the proximity of President René's residence. The barriers are lowered from 6pm onwards. After this all vehicles are checked and only those heading for the Equator or Sheraton hotels on the island's west coast are allowed to proceed.

Some of the island's original cloud forest vegetation still survives around the foot of the Morne Seychellois, part of the large National Park. At

Tea plantation below the Mission Lodge (Mahé)

Mission Lodge, a former Anglican mission school built in 1875, closed in 1889 and today in ruins, there are fine views of the highland landscape and the western coast. Below the Mission are the plantations of the Seychelles Tea Company. The tea-room at the tea factory – soon in view – is an opportunity to enjoy a refreshing break.

Journey resumed, the road winds down the valley of the Desert River past the large State-owned experimental farms to Port Glaud on the coast. A detour north from here leads to Anse l'Islette and the small island to which it owes its name (cross by rowing boat). The road continues across mangrove swamps to La Plaine, but beyond this the north-west tip of Mahé is National Youth Service property (see Art and Culture) and there is no public access.

Returning to Port Glaud take the coast road south, past the Sheraton and Equator hotels. The road cuts through forest for a while before reaching Grand Anse, a huge natural amphitheatre of granite rock where the beach is notorious for its dangerous currents.

At the little township of Grand Anse follow the road which turns inland (unsignposted) to La Misère. Its first sharp bend affords a magnificent view of the islands which lie off Mahé's western coast. Winding its way past the US Receiving Station and the newly established tea and coffee plantations, the road reaches La Misère, a neat and tidy outpost of Victoria. Here a forest track on the right leads up to the US Satellite Tracking Station, its silver domes visible from afar. A parking place on the roadside near by also offers a splendid panorama of Mahé's east coast, from Victoria to the airport. Finally drive back to Victoria, passing a number of restaurants and guest houses on the way.

Walks and Trails

N.B.   Although the Seychelles Tourist Office is making every effort to signpost paths and keep them clear of rampant vegetation, most of the walks and trails are in a fairly poor state and the going is often hard. The Tourist Office also publishes leaflets with advice about walking on the various islands (see Practical Information, Sport, for details of precautions to be taken when walking in the Seychelles).

The walks are graded for difficulty (e for easy, m for moderate, h for hard). Taking a guide – advisable anyway when tackling one of the more difficult routes – is always a good idea, transforming what is otherwise just a walk into an interesting nature study. Guides can be arranged through one of the local tour operators or the Seychelles Tourist Office.

Mahé

1. Coast to coast over the hills of north Mahé:
Start by taking the road (surfaced to begin with) from Anse Étoile, north of Victoria, inland to La Gogue, arriving after about 2km of ascent at the La Gogue Reservoir. Continue along the right-hand side of the reservoir, turning right into woods about 100m before its end. From here it is a further 20 minutes walk to Mont Plaisir (250m), a beautiful vantage point from which to look down on Beau Vallon Bay and across to Silhouette and North Island. The track then descends through coconut groves to Glacis, coming out onto the coast road at the police station, about 200m south of the Visto do Mar Hotel. From here a bus can be caught back to Victoria, either north-bound round the tip of the island or south-bound via Beau Vallon Bay.
Time: 2 hours; grade: e.

2. Beau Vallon or Danzilles to Anse Major:
From Beau Vallon drive or take the bus west along the shores of the bay to Danzilles where the La Scala Restaurant is the starting-point for the walk. Follow the tarred road to its end, beyond which a path, narrow in places, winds at first through dense woodland and then over cliffs to Anse Major. By starting out at about 3.30pm it is possible to watch the sun setting behind Silhouette and still be back at the car before dark. Anyone intending to continue on to Baie Ternay however should make a morning start.
Time: 40 minutes each way; grade: e.

3. Trois Frères Peak and then on to Le Niol:
Take the Sans Souci Road through Victoria's Bel Air suburb, driving past the US Embassy and the "Feba Radio" broadcasting station and on for another 500m to where a sign on the right indicates the start of the walk. A short way along the track there is a place to leave the car – and an already delightful view of Victoria. The path, once used by the workers of a cinnamon plantation, leads steeply up into the forest, sometimes making its way over large boulders. Once out into the open among the rocks (often very slippery after rain) follow the yellow markers. At the top of the pass the route divides, the right-hand track continuing to Trois Frères Peak. The ascent is steep so this particular walk is best started in the early morning or after the worst of the midday heat. The left-hand track goes on to Le Niol where there is the option of taking the road (bus route) back to St Louis or one of the forest paths down to the beach at Bel Ombre or Beau Vallon.
Time: 1½ hours each way from the parking place to the peak, 2 hours from the peak to Le Niol; grade: m to h.

4. Ascent of Morne Blanc:
This walk starts from the tea-room at the tea plantation on the outskirts of Victoria (on the Forêt Noire road; ask someone to point out the precise

place where the hill track leaves the road). The track climbs steeply at first through the tea plantation, then through thick, dank forest to the summit (marked by a triangulation point). Great care is needed here, the crag being precipitous on all sides; so this particular walk is best avoided on overcast or misty days. White tropic birds are a common sight at the top.
Time to the summit: *c.* 1½ hours; grade: m.

5. Val Riche to Mont Copolia:
The walk begins near the "Boathouse", a private house on the Sans Souci/ Forêt Noire road (a boat in the garden accounts for the name). On the left of the road, about 250m beyond the furthest traffic barrier, a route signposted with blue markers slopes down sharply at first into the Val Riche before climbing again through a forest of cinnamon trees, coco plums and palms. Considerable care is needed on reaching the higher altitudes because the blue markers are not always visible and treacherous deeply gaping holes between boulders can often be concealed by the greenery. The reward is a magnificent panorama from the flat granite summit plateau, taking in the east and north coasts of Mahé and the other islands in the group. An additional attraction are the carnivorous pitcher plants, found only at this height.
Time: 1 hour each way; grade: m to h.

6. Round walk from Anse Royale to Anse à la Mouche and back:
From Anse Royale drive (or take the bus) south along the coast to Anse Bougainville. Just after the third bend beyond the Bougainville Guest House a track runs inland, with a sign prohibiting access to vehicles over 3 tonnes. The track is surfaced to its highest point (*c.* 1400m from the coast) but 600m or so beyond it becomes passable only on foot or with a cross-country vehicle. Hidden away up here, well back from the sea, is the Val d'Endor Estate, one of the Seychelles' largest tropical fruit plantations. After another 500m the track improves again and also divides, the right-

Church in Anse Royal (Mahé)

67

Petite Anse Kerlan (Praslin)

hand fork leading to Baie Lazare (3.5km) on the island's western side. From there follow the coast road north for about 4km in the direction of Anse à la Mouche (visiting the artist Michael Adams' studio on the way). A 4km long hill track leads from the Sancta Maria Estate back across the island to Anse Royale. (Alternatively this last stage can be completed by road, taking the bus.)
Time: 1 day; grade: e.

7. Round walk from Baie Lazare to Anse Gaulettes and back:
Take the track which runs inland from the police station in Baie Lazare village, wending its way upwards through beautiful plantation country with, every now and then, a glimpse of the coastal landscape below. After about 3.5km it meets the track from Anse Bougainville which comes over the crest of the island. Turn right here for Anse Gaulettes (1km), afterwards walking back along the main road to Baie Lazare village.
Time: 2 hours; grade: e.

8. Val Mer to Pointe Lazare and back:
From the Hotel Plantation Club a narrow path runs along the shore before plunging into the forest above a small group of huts. Ignore the sign saying "Private Property" where the path starts to descend again (entry is allowed by the German land owner – often away – though any instructions from the estate manager should of course be followed). At the end of the pretty little bay called Petit Gouvernement the path begins to climb once more, coming to an end shortly before a wooden house overlooked on the right by a terrace on a rocky spur. From here there is a fine view back to Baie Lazare, Anse Gaulettes and Pointe Maravi, as well as an opportunity to watch the waves rolling in from the open sea and breaking against the rocks.
Time: 1½ hours there and back; grade: e.

Praslin

On Praslin the circular walk round the Vallée de Mai National Park (see The Seychelles from A to Z) is especially recommended . Additionally there are two lovely walks through the interior of the island which can be combined to make a round walk.

1. From Anse Kerlan to Anse Lazio:
Starting from Grand Anse or from the airport take the bus to Anse Kerlan in the north-west of the island. From there follow the coast road to a fork beyond the poultry farm. A narrow track continuing left towards the sea makes a thoroughly delightful detour to Anse Kerlan and Petite Anse Kerlan, two crescent shaped beaches back-to-back, separated only by the rocky cliffs of Pointe St Marie. Alternatively branch right along the white cement road through the forest, arriving after a few hundred metres at a small settlement. Here a footpath crosses the hills to a bay called Anse Lazio, with a small community of the same name. The beach at Anse Lazio is the loveliest on Praslin. From Anse Lazio follow the road down the island's eastern side to Anse Volbert village, either on foot or taking the bus from Anse Boudin.
Time: 3 hours; grade: e.

2. From Anse Volbert to Grand Anse:
This walk follows the coast road from Anse Volbert village northwards to Anse Petite Cour and from there to Anse Possession. At Anse Possession the Pasquière Track turns off left (just past a small bridge) and crosses the island. It comes out at the Britannia Restaurant in Grand Anse.
Time: 2 hours; grade: e.

The Seychelles from A to Z

African Banks

See Amirantes – Les Amirantes, African Banks, St Joseph (Atoll), Poivre (Atoll)

Aldabra (Atoll)

Area: 153.8sq.km
Population: c. 15

Special permission is required for a visit to Aldabra. It can only be reached on the supply ship "Cinq Juin" (which calls in every two to three months) or by chartered schooner.

Getting there

The atoll lies 400km from the northern tip of Madagascar and 650km from the coast of Tanzania (9°22' to 9°30'S 46°12' to 46°32'E). It is 1160km from Mahé.

The island group was almost certainly known to the Arabs as early as the 9th or 10th c. They called it "al khadra" ("the green one"), which the Portuguese later rendered "Al Hadara". This in turn went through a succession of changes – D'Arena, Y d'Ared, Illharada – before finally becoming Aldabra.
The Portuguese navigator Vasco da Gama landed here in 1502 or 1503 while on his second voyage to India. The islands were first settled in 1899 at which time the coconut plantations were established (one plantation, almost 3km long, survives on Grande Terre).

History and origin of the name

Description of the atoll

Aldabra is 35km long, 13km wide and has a total area (including the lagoon) of 365sq.km, making it the largest atoll in the world. Its land area

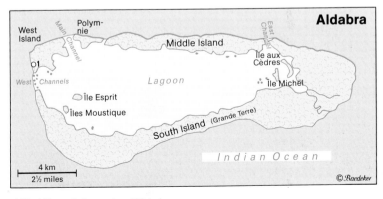

◀ Clock Tower in the centre of Victoria

Giant tortoises on Aldabra

(153.8sq.km) is exactly the same as that of Mahé, the principal island in the Seychelles. The atoll is split up into a number of different islands: Grand Terre (English: South Island), Île Picard (English: West Island), Polymnie, Île Malabar or Moyenne (English: Middle Island), Île aux Cèdres, Île Michel, Île Esprit, Îles Moustique, Îlot Parc, Îlot Émile, Îlot Yangue, Îlot Dubois, Îlot Magnan and Île Lanier, together with numerous islets and reefs.

Among scientists Aldabra is considered the most interesting of the islands in the Indian Ocean on account of its unique biological nature. The atoll is probably about 80,000 years old, formed over millennia from coral reefs which became established on the rim of a submerged volcanic crater. The lagoon, fringed with mangrove swamps, is linked in four places to the open sea by channels through the ring of coral. Water streams into the lagoon with the rising tide, flowing out again with the ebb to leave the coral beds almost dry.

Aldabra's unique flora and fauna owe their survival largely to its isolation, an isolation threatened on a number of occasions this century by schemes to exploit the atoll for economic (guano) or military purposes. British plans to establish a military base on Aldabra were only halted when the Labour government decided in 1971 to withdraw all British forces from east of Suez.

The chief islands of the Aldabra Atoll consist of coral banks up to 8m high, covered by sand dunes which can reach heights of as much as 30m.

Giant tortoises

Aldabra is the true home of the giant tortoise, creatures which in earlier times were callously slaughtered for their tasty meat. On a single expedition in 1842 as many as 1200 are believed to have been rounded up by the crews of just two ships and taken to Mauritius for processing. By the turn of the century Aldabra's tortoises appear to have been close to extinction, but thanks to strict conservation measures the species has been able to multiply again.

Zoologists estimate that between 150,000 and 180,000 tortoises are now living on the atoll, where they have no natural enemies. The Galapagos Islands are the only other part of the world where giant tortoises, which cannot tolerate strong sunlight or large temperature fluctuations, are still found in large numbers.

Giant tortoises feed mainly on grasses. Those living on the other islands in the Seychelles have been taken there from Aldabra.

Between December and March the islands of the atoll are visited by a great many varieties of turtle, all of which come to bury their eggs in the fine shelly sand. Aldabra is also home to between 6000 and 7000 white rails, the Indian Ocean's sole surviving species of flightless bird. They are not unlike the now extinct but legendary dodo from Mauritius.

Turtles and white rails

Innumerable birds of passage including herons, flamingoes and terns regularly visit the atoll on migration.

Aldabra was declared a nature reserve in 1968 and since 1979 has been administered by the Seychelles Island Foundation. In 1983 it was listed as a "world heritage site" by the United Nations. There is a biological research station on the island of Picard at the atoll's western end.

Nature reserve

Alphonse, Bijoutier, St François (Atoll)

Area: 1.98sq.km (Alphonse 1.74sq.km, Bijoutier 0.07sq.km, St François 0.17sq.km)
Inhabitants: a few

Alphonse (7° to 7°20′S 52°50′E) lies about 400km south of Mahé (see entry) and about 90km south of the outermost island in the Amirantes group (see entry). It is a coral island and considered by some experts to be properly part of the Amirantes group.

Location and general

Located immediately to the south are the island of Bijoutier and the St François atoll. Alphonse has a small landing strip.

The island was named after Chevalier Alphonse de Pontevez, commander of the French frigate "Lys", who was the first to land there in 1730.

History and origin of the name

Amirantes – Les Amirantes, African Banks, St Joseph (Atoll), Poivre (Atoll)

Area: 9.23sq.km (Amirantes 6.61sq.km, African Banks, St Joseph 1.22sq.km, Poivre 1.1sq.km)
Population: 100–150

There are landing strips for small aircraft on the islands of Desroches, D'Arros, Rémire and Marie Louise.

Flights

The islands of the Amirantes group, together with the African Banks, St Joseph Atoll and Poivre Atoll, are situated between latitude 4°50′ and 6°30′S and longitude 53° and 53°40′E. They lie south-west of the main Seychelles group, between 200 and 340km from Mahé.

Location and general

The true Amirantes comprise the islands of D'Arros (Darros; 1.5sq.km), Rémire (Eagle; 0.27sq.km), Boudeuse (0.01sq.km), Desnœufs (0.35sq.km), Desroches (3.94sq.km), Étoile (Lampéraire; 0.01sq.km) and Marie Louise (0.52sq.km). Spread over a distance of some 150km they are part of a

73

Amirantes – Les Amirantes, African Banks, St Joseph (Atoll), Poivre (Atoll)

A bird's-eye view of Desroches

submarine ridge which extends from the Mahé group southwards to Mauritius and Réunion.

Nesting site for terns

During the northern summer the Amirantes and the neighbouring islands are a breeding ground for hundreds of thousands of terns.

Economy

Up to now only Desroches has seen any economic development, boasting a copra factory and a recently built hotel (with chalet accommodation). Desroches copra is considered the best produced in the Indian Ocean region and is consequently very much in demand.

History and origin of the names

The Amirantes – from "Ilhas do Almirante" (Admiral Islands) – were discovered and christened by Vasco da Gama while on his second voyage to India in 1502 or 1503. The African Banks or "Îlots Africains" were named in 1792 by the French Admiral Willaumez flying his flag in "La Régénérée". Boudeuse and Etoile took their names from two of the ships belonging to Louis Antoine de Bougainville (1729–1811) who, between 1766 and 1769, became the first Frenchman to circumnavigate the globe.
D'Arros was named after Baron D'Arros, Marine Commandant of the Île de France (Mauritius) from 1770 to 1771. Desroches in turn was named after the man who was Governor of the Île de France from 1767 to 1772 (by Chevalier de la Biollière who first explored the island in 1771). Also in 1771 the island of Marie Louise was given its name by Chevalier de Roslan.

Watersports

The only hotel – still relatively new – is on Desroches (flights from Mahé on Mondays, Wednesdays and Saturdays, taking about 40 minutes). The company which manages the hotel also runs the island's watersports centre. In contrast to most of the other coral islands there is no lack of hot water on Desroches because of its very efficient sea water treatment plant.

Preparatory work for copra production

Aride – Île Aride

Area: 0.68sq.km
Population: 10

It is only possible to visit Aride between 1st October and 30th April. At other times the heavy swell makes landing by boat difficult if not impossible. **N.B.**

Day trips (landing fee) are organised from Mahé (2 hour crossing) and from Praslin (45 minute crossing).

Aride (4°12′S 55°40′E) is the most northerly of the granite islands on the Seychelles Plateau. It lies some 54km north-east of Mahé and 10km north of Praslin. It is 1.6km long and 0.6km wide. Location

Partly encircled by a fringing coral reef Aride rises to a height of 152m above sea level. It is covered with lush, tropical vegetation the richness of which makes the island a continuing focus of botanical interest. It is now virtually the only place in the world where the delicate, white blooms of Wright's gardenia can still be found. In addition to rare plants, tropical fruits and spices also grow in profusion, among them papayas, guavas, ginger, lemons, cinnamon trees, oranges, grapefruit, pumpkin and bananas.
The island is privately owned. It has been declared a nature reserve and is watched over by a British conservation society. Terrain and plant life

Huts clustering round the beach at the landing place are the homes of the island's few inhabitants, and make up the tiny settlement of La Cour. Spices used to be grown on the narrow flat coastal strip. Inhabitants

Aride was discovered in 1756 by Captain Nicolas Morphey and was originally called "Île Moras" after the French Minister of Marine. Being so hot and dry it later became known as Aride. History and origin of the name

75

As on other islands there are many tales of pirates and hidden treasure on Aride. A few years ago a human – probably African – skeleton, buried in a sitting position, was accidentally uncovered.

Sea birds

As well as its giant millipedes and its coots with shimmering bluish feathers, Aride has the largest colony of sea birds of all the granite islands. These include nesting white or fairy terns, sooty or wide-awake terns, noddys and roseate terns, the great frigate bird, and the red-tailed tropic bird whose nests can be observed on the island's highest point – Gros la Tête (134m above sea level).

Mapou tree

Also to be seen on Aride's hillside is the mapou tree, which sheds its leaves continuously throughout the year. The layer of humus which results can reach the impressive depth of half a metre within a period of only 20 or 30 years.

Assomption – Assumption

Area: 1.17sq.km
Inhabitants: a manager and one or two workers

Location and general

Assomption (or Assumption) lies *c.* 1200km south-west of Mahé (9°44'S 46°30'E), not far from Aldabra Atoll. It was once among the world's most important breeding sites for many different varieties of sea bird. Since 1840, however, more than a million tonnes of guano – used as fertiliser on the sugar cane plantations of Mauritius and a major contributor to the Seychelles's balance of trade – have been removed from the island, with complete disregard for the consequential destruction of the birds' natural habitat.

Astove

Area: 6.61sq.km
Inhabitants: a few

Location and general

Astove (10°4'S 47°44'E) is situated about 40km south-east of Cosmoledo (see entry). The two are sometimes regarded as forming an island group. Astove is managed by the state-run Islands Development Company, which quarries the guano and maintains a landing strip for small aircraft.

Bijoutier

See Alphonse, Bijoutier, St François (Atoll)

Bird Island – Île aux Vaches Marines

Area: 1.01sq.km
Population: 45

Flights and accommodation

The only habitation on privately owned Bird Island is a hotel (with bungalow accommodation). There are daily flights from Mahé taking 30 to 40 minutes. Seats on the chartered plane are only available to those booked into the hotel for at least one night.

Leisure and sport

The waters around Bird Island, being rich in corals and fish, are ideal for diving and deep-sea angling. The white sand beaches of powdered shell and coral and the crystal-clear sea make sunbathing and swimming just as inviting.

Bird Island (3°43'S 55°13'E) lies just 100km north of Mahé. It is on the very edge of the Mahé Plateau which drops away almost immediately to depths of 1800m. Its sister island, Denis, is about 50km away to the east.

Location

From a geological point of view the flat, palm-covered Bird Island belongs with the outlying coral islands (as does Denis Island too). It is counted part of the main island group purely on account of its location. Bird, formed by deposits of sand and muschelkalk building up on a coral reef, rises only a few dozen centimetres above sea level. It is 1.52km long and 0.64km wide.

Terrain and general

The island owes its luxuriant vegetation to a thick layer of guano. This natural fertiliser, rich in nitrogen and phosphates, comes from the excrement and other deposits left behind by the huge bird colonies.

Thick swathes of coconut palms grow all around the island, while papayas, mangoes and avocados thrive in the plantations. All the produce of the island's farm – including vegetables, eggs, chicken and pork – goes towards supplying the needs of the hotel.

Bird Island's low topography means that it is spared the orographic rainfall typical of the more mountainous granite islands. As a result the island is drier and has far more reliable sunny weather than either Mahé or Praslin.

Climate

The water supply on Bird comes from two different sources. Water for general use is pumped up from below the sand, tapping the freshwater bubble which "floats" on the salt water beneath. This water is very brackish and as the salt would very quickly corrode any heating system the island has no hot water supply. Drinking water is provided by rainwater collected in large cisterns.

Sea birds on the beach of Bird Island

Bird Island – Île aux Vaches Marines

History and origin of the name

The island was discovered in 1756 by Nicolas Morphey who christened it "Île aux Vaches Marines" – "Sea-Cow Island" – because of the dugongs there (these animals are now extinct in the Seychelles). The name is still used occasionally in official documents.

The name "Bird Island", which reflects the fact that the island shelters millions of sea birds for many months in the year, was first used in 1771 by a cartographer aboard the British ship "The Fireworker".

*Sea birds and tortoises

Sea birds

A bird sanctuary in the north-east corner of the island is home to millions of terns. Sea birds – huge flocks of sooty terns, white or fairy terns, noddys, crested, little and swift terns as well as sandpipers, frigate birds and tropic birds – are, in fact, the island's real attraction, especially during the European summer. They are seen here in their natural habitat; some are so tame that an observer can be almost within touching distance before they fly away.

Every year between April and October as many as one to two million sooty terns visit the bird sanctuary to breed and raise their young before returning to the open sea. They are thought to spend the rest of the year completely out of touch with land (this being confirmed by the fact that no sightings of these sooty terns have ever been reported from elsewhere).

Tortoises

Although once very numerous there are now only two giant tortoises on the island, and both of these were brought in from Aldabra. The male, called "Esmeralda", is 150 to 200 years old with a shell more than 1.80m in length – reputedly the oldest tortoise in the world as well as the largest.

"Esmeralda", a giant tortoise on Bird Island

78

Cerf Island – Île au Cerf

Area: 1.27sq.km
Population: *c.* 40

Excursion boats make the 10 to 15 minute crossing from Victoria (Mahé). There is no hotel but the island does have a bar and a restaurant.

Getting there

Cerf Island lies off Mahé's east coast, in Victoria bay. It is only 4km east of the harbour at Victoria, and 2.5km offshore.

Location

The privately owned island, 1.7km long by 0.9km wide, is part of the Sainte Anne Marine National Park. It is 108m above sea level at its highest point. Although only a few families live on the island it has two chapels, one Anglican and one Catholic. The inhabitants make a living by growing fruit and vegetables and from coconuts.

Terrain and general

The island was discovered in 1742 by Lazare Picault on his first voyage to the Seychelles. It was named in 1756 by Captain Nicolas Morphey after the frigate "Le Cerf" ("The Stag") under his command.

History and origin of the name

As well as being the home of a number of giant tortoises Cerf also has one or two colonies of flying foxes. The island's beaches are visited regularly by turtles coming to lay their eggs in the sand.

Fauna

Cerf can easily be walked round in two or three hours. A path from the pier leads between the two hills in the centre of the island, to the bay at the south end where there is good bathing and snorkelling.

Round walk

Coëtivy Island

Area: 9.32sq.km
Inhabitants: none

Coëtivy, about 270km south of Mahé, is the most easterly island in the Seychelles (7°20'S 56°15'E). Like Île Plate it stands alone, not being part of any island group.
The island was named after Chevalier de Coëtivy who sighted it for the first time on 3rd July, 1771 whilst aboard his ship the "Île de France". Visitors are not permitted.

Location and general

Conception

Area: 0.6sq.km
Inhabitants: none

Excursion boats from Beau Vallon Bay (Mahé) make occasional visits to the island.

Getting there

Conception (1.5km long by 0.5km wide) lies about 1.5km off the entrance to Port Launay bay at the north-western tip of Mahé, separated from Mahé by a channel called "La Passe Ternay". The most distinctive feature of the island is a hilly ridge which extends for more than a hundred metres and is 100m above sea level at its highest point.

Location and general

Cosmoledo (Atoll)

Area: 5.09sq.km
Inhabitants: none

Cousin Island

Location and general | Cosmoledo Atoll (9°30′S 47°30′ to 47°40′E) is situated some 1050km south-west of Mahé. It is made up of a number of separate islands – Menai, Île du Nord, Île Nord-Est, Île du Trou, Goëlette, Grand Polyte, Petite Polyte, Grand Île (Wizard), Pagode, Île du Sud, Île Moustiques, Île Baleine and Île Chauve Souris. A huge variety of different sea birds, including a great many gannets, make their home on Cosmoledo. Every year innumerable turtles also come ashore to lay their eggs on the island's sandy beaches.

Cousin Island

Area: 0.29sq.km
Population: 5

When to go | Cousin is best visited in April and May – at the height of the breeding season for the 250,000 or so birds which nest there.

Getting there | Boats sail for Cousin from Praslin on Tuesdays, Thursdays and Fridays. Visitors must be accompanied by a guide; numbers are restricted to twenty people visiting the island at any one time.

Sport | Visitors to the island are only allowed to swim on one small stretch of beach, and then only with the agreement of the warden.

Location and general | Cousin Island is situated some 3km off the settlement of Amitié on Praslin (see entry), 36km north-east of Mahé and 12km south of Aride. The island is 0.8km long and 0.6km wide. Its highest point is 66m above sea level.

*Birdlife

Cousin is one of the most interesting of all the islands in the Seychelles. Since 1968 it has belonged to the International Council for Bird Preservation and is a nature reserve.

One priority has been to provide a suitable habitat on the island for a number of rare endemic bird species threatened with extinction, among them the Seychelles brush warbler, the Seychelles warbler and the Seychelles fody. As a result of the stringently enforced conservation measures – e.g. strict control of the number of visitors, a ban on any form of economic development, and keeping the island free of rats and domestic animals – these species have been able to multiply in a relatively short time from just a small number of individuals to quite sizeable populations.

In addition to the species already mentioned Cousin Island is the haunt of moorhens, zebra doves, turnstones, Seychelles sunbirds and Madagascar fodys. There are also quite large colonies of various types of sea bird including the white-tailed tropic bird (whose nests can be seen on the ground in sheltered spots all over the island), the wedge-tailed and the Audubon's shearwater and the sooty and the white tern.

Ghost crabs | Hoards of ghost crabs (*Ocypodes sp.*) inhabit Cousin's beaches. During the mating season the male crabs vibrate their pincers, producing a weird sound not unlike the shrilling and rasping of the short-horned grasshopper.

Cousine Island

Area: 0.26sq.km
Inhabitants: none

A young white-tailed tropical bird (Cousin Island)

Cousine lies about 2km south-east of Cousin Island (see entry) and 5km off Praslin's western coast. The privately owned island, 1km long and 0.4km wide, is not accessible to the public.

Location and general

Curieuse Island – Île Curieuse

Area: 2.86sq.km
Inhabitants: the warden and his family

Boat trips to Curieuse Island run almost daily from Praslin.

Getting there

The waters around Curieuse (the Curieuse Marine National Park) are a rich exploration ground for divers and snorkellers.

Sport

Curieuse is situated immediately north-east of Praslin (see entry), separated by the waters of Curieuse Bay. At Anse Boudin (on Praslin's coast) the bay is just 1km across. The island is 44km from Victoria.

Location

Curieuse, discovered by Lazare Picault in 1744, was christened some years later, by Marion Dufresne (after one of the ships on his 1768 expedition). In 1771 sailors from the corvette "Eagle" set the island ablaze – the intention being to make the task of harvesting coco de mer nuts, the fruit of the coco de mer palm, easier. As a result most of the unique palms, found only here and on nearby Praslin, were destroyed. From 1833 onwards there was a leper colony on the island, continuing, with some interruptions, until 1965. The doctor's house, where the warden now lives, is the only building to survive intact.

History and origin of the name

From having been very similar to Praslin the interior of Curieuse was left almost completely denuded of vegetation by the conflagration in 1771.

Flora and fauna

81

Only a very few coco de mer palms survived the ecological disaster. Attempts are now being made to re-introduce the trees in greater numbers. A colony of almost 250 giant tortoises were brought from Aldabra some years ago and are now well established. The island is part of the Curieuse National Park.

Denis Island

Area: 1.43sq.km
Population: 55

Flights

There are flights daily from Mahé (taking about 50 minutes) on Wednesdays, Fridays and Sundays. The planes are chartered from Air Seychelles and seats are restricted to those with a hotel booking.

By boat

The supply boat from Mahé provides an irregular service to the island.

Sport

Windsurfing, snorkelling, sailing and diving are all catered for. Off the island's west coast the coral reef, which completely encircles Denis, drops away sharply to depths of 15 or 30m. The edge of the Seychelles Plateau is also only 8km away and care is sometimes needed in view of the very heavy swell.

Time

Denis Island does not keep normal Seychelles time, clocks being advanced one hour.

Location and general

The island lies about 90km north of Mahé and 50km east of Bird Island (3°48'S 55°40'E).

The half-moon shaped Denis is 1.81km long, 1.3km wide, and only 3.5m above sea level at its highest point. Like its neighbour Bird it is a coral

Denis Island

Settlement on Denis Island

island. Because of its location, however, geologists group it together with the granite islands of the Seychelles (or Mahé) Plateau, on the northern edge of which it stands.

A dense canopy of palms interspersed with casuarinas and takamaka trees covers the entire island.

Denis is privately-owned, belonging to the Seychelles Coconut Estates which also run the hotel (bungalow accommodation once again).

There is a farm on the island which, depending on the season, supplies between 30 and 80% of the fresh food needed by the hotel and its staff. Despite careful management the island's coconut palm plantations and copra factory are barely profitable.

As on Bird Island supplies of drinking water depend on a rainwater cistern, while water for other uses is pumped from the freshwater bubble beneath the sand.

Water supply

Denis Island was discovered on 11th August 1773 by Denis de Trobriant. Early this century coconut plantations were established and guano began to be quarried for fertiliser production (the reserves of guano are now largely exhausted). Cotton has been cultivated from time to time too. Today the island's only significant source of income is the hotel, opened in 1976.

History and origin of the name

What to see

Towering high in the middle of the old plantation is a gas powered lighthouse built in 1910, still sending out its warning signal every five seconds. From the top a splendid panorama unfolds, over Denis itself and across to Praslin and Mahé. Huddling close by the lighthouse is the island's little village, complete with two jail houses.

In the centre of the island stands a small ecumenical chapel in which services are still occasionally held.

A considerable number of giant tortoises live in the wild at the south end of the island, where the beaches are also regularly visited by female turtles coming ashore to lay their eggs.

Farquhar (Atoll), St Pierre, Providence (Atoll)

Area: 11.94sq.km (Farquhar Atoll 7.99sq.km, Saint Pierre 1.67sq.km, Providence 0.57sq.km, Bancs Providence 0.71sq.km)
Population: 100

| Flights | The only landing strip is at Île du Nord, part of the Farquhar Atoll. |

Location

The island group, comprising Farquhar Atoll, St Pierre, Providence Atoll and the Bancs Providence, lies approximately on longitude 51°E and extends between latitudes 9° and 10°10'S. It is 700 to 790km south-west of Mahé (see entry). Farquhar is only 280km from the north coast of Madagascar.

History and naming of the islands

The first European to land on Farquhar was the Portuguese Juan de Nova in 1501 or 1502, and the atoll initially bore his name. It was renamed in 1824 (after the Governor of Mauritius, Sir Robert Townsend Farquhar).
St Pierre on the other hand was not discovered until much later, by Duchemin in 1732. It was named after one of his ships.

Farquhar

The atoll consists of a number of separate islands: Île du Nord, Île du Sud, Manaha Nord, Manaha Milieu, Manaha Sud, Goëlettes, Lapin, Île du Milieu, Depose and Bancs de Sable.
Farquhar's scenery is dominated by palms and casuarinas, the inhabitants making a living from copra and fishing. This is in contrast to St Pierre where the islanders exist by quarrying guano.

*Beach

Farquhar is blessed with one of the most beautiful beaches in the whole of the Seychelles, the 2km long Twenty-Five Franc Beach with sand as fine as flour.
The atoll is a much visited breeding ground for migratory birds and terns.

Félicité

Area: 2.68sq.km
Population: 12

Getting there

Boats sail to Félicité from La Digue and Praslin, from where trips are also organised by local tour operators.

Accommodation

A pair of Seychelles-style dwellings provide accommodation for holiday-makers on Félicité. They are managed by the La Digue Island Lodge.

Location and general

Félicité (4°20'S 55°52'E), one of the islands in the Praslin group, lies between La Digue and Marianne (see entries). It is 55km from Mahé.
The privately owned island, 227m above sea level at its highest point, has no beach. It is covered with coconut palms and tropical trees and surrounded by a cluster of smaller islands (Cocos, Grande Sœur, Petite Sœur and Marianne).

History

In 1875 the Sultan of Perak, part of the Federation of Malaysia, was exiled to Félicité. He lived there in the company of two escorting officers until 1879.

Frégate – Frigate

Area: 2.19sq.km
Population: 30

There is one 25-minute flight a day to Frégate from Mahé. The island can be explored on a day's excursion. — Flights

There are boats to Frégate at irregular intervals from Victoria. The crossing takes about 4 to 5 hours. — By boat

The island's only hotel was built in 1973. While not the most comfortable, its idyllic setting between the beach and the tropical forest make it a perfect spot for relaxation. — Accommodation

Frégate (Frigate) lies a bare 50km east of Mahé and 25km south of La Digue (4°35'S 55°51'E). — Location and general

Once a pirate's lair the island has superb long and lonely sandy beaches and densely wooded hills up to 125m high.

Frégate's vegetation numbers almost 200 different species, nearly all of which are imported "exotic" varieties. They include the tropical cashew or anacardium tree (of which the cashew nut is the seed), citrus fruit, mangoes and Indian almonds. — Flora

The island also has an exceedingly diverse fauna. The Seychelles magpie robin is unique to Frégate, a ground dwelling bird found mainly at higher altitudes (just nineteen individuals are known to survive at the present time). The Seychelles weaver is another rare bird native to the island. Some of the hundred or so giant tortoises – brought from Aldabra more than 40 years ago – are estimated to be over 150 years old. There are also a number of unusual insects, including the huge tenebrionid beetle and giant spiders (completely harmless, however). — Fauna

The soil in the north-east of the island is fertile and phosphate-rich indicating that this must once have been a nesting ground for large colonies of sea birds.

Lazare Picault explored Frégate on his second expedition in 1744, christening it "Île aux Frégates" on account of the frigate birds nesting there. In the — History and origin of the name

85

early 18th c. the island became a pirate stronghold, providing food and water and a base from which to launch their raids. James Bond's creator Ian Fleming was among those convinced that pirate treasure is hidden somewhere on Frégate (a belief supported by various finds such as axes and storage vessels).

In 1801 a number of exiled Jacobins were briefly incarcerated on the island together with three slaves. They were later transported to the Comoros Islands, only to be poisoned there on the orders of the Sultan.

A walk round the island

This walk round the island, following marked nature trails, is thoroughly recommended. Start at the landing strip, going through the plantation in the direction of Anse Parc. The well-beaten path to this magnificent beach will be seen branching off the main track and into a large palm grove. Afterwards the walk resumes on the wider track, leading to a little group of huts beyond which it begins to climb. Shaded by a sometimes dense canopy of leaves, follow the black arrows marking the route over the rocks. As the vegetation becomes lower, La Digue comes into view in the distance on the right. The track then climbs gently over further rocky terrain until, after a few hundred metres, it ducks under a canopy of green once more and starts its descent towards the beach at Grand Anse. (This part of the walk takes about an hour.)

Continue along the beach until a hut is seen behind bushes on the right. Here a track climbs steeply up the hillside to where a path branches off left to a crater-shaped water-filled basin in the granite rock. Watch for a magpie robin among the birds pottering about its rim. After this the main track goes down hill again to the plantation. An alternative is to continue along Grand

Anse Parc, in the south of Frégate Island

Anse Bamboo, with rounded granite cliffs (Frégate)

Anse beach to its northern end where a narrow path leads to one of the very best bathing beaches anywhere in the Seychelles, Anse Victoria at the north of the island. From here a direct though sometimes rocky track returns to Plantation House, taking about 25 minutes.

Anse Parc and Grand Anse in the south of the island are ideal for snorkelling when the tide is in (at low tide the water is too shallow). Anse Bamboo – at the north end of the landing strip – is one of the island's most scenic spots, its granite cliffs worn smooth by the sea. Dangerous currents make it unsuitable for bathing, however.

Bays

Grande Sœur, Petite Sœur

Area: 0.84sq.km
Inhabitants: none

There are boat trips from Praslin to Grande Sœur.

Getting there

Grande Sœur, with its sister island Petite Sœur (one-third the size), is 56km from Mahé, situated 18 to 20km east of Praslin and 4km north of Félicité. The two islands, also known as "Les Sœurs", are uninhabited. Banks of coral make the channel between Grande and Petite Sœurs a particular favourite with divers.

Location and general

La Digue

Area: 10.1sq.km
Population: *c.* 2500

La Digue

Getting there
The "Lady Mary", "La Silhouette", and "L'Ideal" provide a boat service to La Digue from the pier at Praslin's Baie Ste Anne, leaving several times a day. Depending on the weather the crossing takes 20 to 30 minutes. There are also sailings to La Digue from Mahé (either direct or via Praslin) aboard the "Arctic Tern", "La Belle Edna" and "La Belle Vue" which carry freight as well as passengers.

Local transport
Apart from a few buses belonging to local tour operators the only means of transport on the island are ox carts or bicycles (which can be hired at the pier at La Passe or in La Réunion). All the island's beaches are within easy reach of the pier or the hotel by bicycle or on foot.

Sport
There is good diving to be found practically anywhere in the waters around La Digue, the best being in the vicinity of the Ave Maria Rocks (2km south) and the Channel Rocks (between La Digue and Round Island, an islet off Praslin's south-east coast). There is also excellent snorkelling in the bay at Anse Patates, at Anse La Réunion on the west coast (opposite the island hotel), and – in calm weather – in the bays at Anse Cocos, Petite Anse and

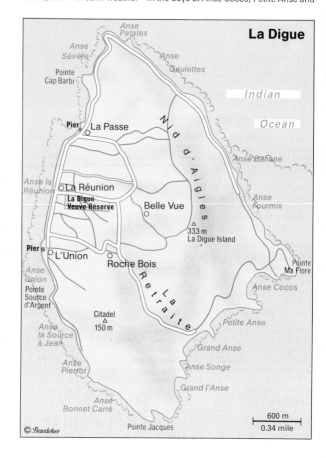

Grand Anse (on the east coast). The hotel caters for other kinds of water-sports as well (e.g. water skiing and sailing).

La Digue (4°20' to 4°23'S 55°50' to 55°52'E) is one of the group of islands which surround Praslin (see entry) from which it is separated by a channel only 5km wide.

The island, c. 5km long and 3km wide, is the fourth largest on the Seychelles Plateau. It is generally considered the most beautiful of all the islands in the Seychelles.

Annual precipitation on the low-lying La Digue is considerably less than on Mahé (where much of the rainfall results from moist air being forced upwards over the higher ground). La Digue's average monthly rainfall is only c. 150mm. The water supply relies on groundwater, normally sufficient although there are occasional shortages.

Lacking the protection of an offshore coral reef the island's east coast can be subject to heavy swell during the south-east monsoon, making it sometimes dangerous for bathing or snorkelling.

La Digue was discovered by Lazare Picault in 1744 and was originally christened "Île Rouge" from the reddish colour of its granite rocks. At sunset these can turn a really deep shade of red.

Duchemin, who commanded the two ships of Marion Dufresne's 1768 expedition, renamed the island after his flagship "La Digue".

The island landscape

Whether on the coast or inland, houses and little huts nestle singly or in smallish groups, often hidden in the dense foliage of tropical vegetation

A colonial house in La Réunion

La Digue

Beach at the Petite Anse of La Digue

which includes trees a century old or more. The island has two "centres", La Réunion and – just 1km of a mile to the north – La Passe, a little settlement built around the pier. Both are on the west side and neither boasts more than a handful of dwellings, a shop, a church and a couple of buildings housing the post-office, etc. La Réunion also has a hotel.

*Rocks and
*beaches

Especially in the south of the island interesting rock formations follow close one upon another, along the coast and also inland where they tower up to 333m high. Anse La Réunion, on the west side, is the island's longest beach. Among the favourite haunts of tourists and commercial photographers from all over the world are Grand Anse, Petite Anse and Anse Cocos on the east side, and Anse la Source à Jean with the nearby rock cliffs of Pointe Source d'Argent on the west (1.5km south of the settlement at La Réunion). The loveliest bay at the north end of the island is the isolated Anse Patates where tall waves sweeping in from the open sea break on the red granite rocks.

A walk round the island

All La Digue's most important "sights" are encompassed by this walk round the island, which can be done in less than a day. Starting from the pier at La Passe first follow the road southwards to La Réunion where the island's only hotel (apart from one or two rather simple guest houses) will be found. There is a small supermarket opposite the hotel's main entrance, a good place to buy something to eat on the walk. St Mary's Church, the largest on the island, is also worth a visit. From here the road continues south towards Anse Union where the President of the Seychelles elects to spend his weekends and holidays. The copra factory still operates and can be visited (weekdays only). A few metres past the farm buildings of the copra factory stands an impressive granite rock with sea anemones decorating the pool at its foot.

Anse la Source à Jean on the west coast

Continue south along the beach until the narrow path winds round the granite boulders at Pointe Source d'Argent to another beach at Anse La Source à Jean.

**Pointe Source d'Argent

Now return to the church at La Réunion. Here a wide road heads inland, skirting (for almost 1km) the nature reserve established specifically for the Seychelles paradise flycatcher (or paradise whydah). The reserve (La Digue Veuve Réserve) was set up jointly by the Seychelles National Commission for the Environment and the British Royal Society for Nature Conservation in an attempt to save the rare bird from extinction by protecting one of its last remaining habitats.

*Nature reserve

A number of other species of land bird typical of the Seychelles can also be seen in the reserve, including the bulbul, the sunbird, the Madagascar turtle dove, the Madagascar weaver and the Indian rose-coloured starling.

The road climbs here, but only gently. At the first fork branch off right towards a small hill in the centre of the island. On the far side of the hill a quite modern looking experimental farm can be seen below the road, which then continues to the bay at Grand Anse.

From Grand Anse a path strikes off over the rocky cliffs behind the beach, leading first to Petite Anse and then Anse Cocos. The track then goes round Pointe Ma Flore towards the north end of the island, passing Anse Fourmis, Anse Banane and (now on a surfaced road) Anse Patates at the most northerly tip. From there it is barely 1.5km by road past Anse Sévère and round Pointe Cap Barbi back to the pier. Proceeding at a leisurely walking pace but allowing for only brief halts at the beaches it is possible to get all round the island comfortably in a day.

To visit the island's highest point, the summit of Nid d'Aigles (the eagles' nest), take the dust road which leads from the pier directly into the interior.

Nid d'Aigles

L'Islette

At the landing-stage of La Passe

After *c.* 2km turn off left along a track, at a property which goes under the splendid name of "Château". The whole ascent takes about an hour.

L'Islette

Area: 0.03sq.km
Inhabitants: hotel and restaurant staff

Getting there

Visitors are ferried across from Mahé in a small motor boat belonging to the L'Islette Guest House. Arrangements can be made in advance by telephone or the boat summoned simply by a call and wave from the shore.

Location and general

L'Islette lies between the islands of Mahé and Thérèse (see entries), sheltered by Anse L'Islette's protective barrier of coral.

Only about 300m from the Mahé shore, the tiny island has a guest house and restaurant.

Long Island – Île Longue

Area: 0.21sq.km
Inhabitants: none

Location and general

Long Island, one of the islands in the bay of Victoria, is *c.* 0.4km from Moyenne (see entry), 0.5km from Cerf Island (see entry) and 5km from Victoria itself. Like its immediate neighbours it is part of the Sainte Anne Marine National Park.

The 0.8 by 0.3km island was christened in 1742 by the man who discovered it, Lazare Picault. It is now the site of a prison and is not accessible to the public.

Mahé

Area: 152.52sq.km (plus 1.24sq.km of reclaimed land)
Population: 59,060
Principal town: Victoria (capital of the Republic of Seychelles)

About 85% of the 3600 (minimum) tourist beds available in the Seychelles are located on the principal island of Mahé, as are all the hotels with more than 40 rooms (the majority of which are concentrated on the north-west coast between Bel Ombre, Beau Vallon Bay and Glacis). Mahé's second most important tourist centre is on the island's west side, around Grand Anse and Port Glaud. The south-east coast has one large hotel (with golf course) and several small guest houses, but no bathing beach worth mentioning. The south-west in contrast boasts some of the best beaches and offers one or two really comfortable hotels and guest houses, as well as a number of good restaurants.

Tourist centre

There is a good selection of entertainment available on Mahé over and above enjoyment of the beaches and watersports. The hotels, for example, organise dancing in the evenings, and there are casinos (foreigners only) at the Beau Vallon Bay Hotel and the Plantation Club.

Leisure and sport

Mahé lies between 4°33' and 4°48'S and between 55°23' and 55°32'E. It is about 1580km from the Kenyan port of Mombasa and 2800km from Bombay on the west coast of India. The islands of the Amirantes group are some 300km distant, the Farquhar group 800km, and Aldabra Atoll 1100km.

Location

Mahé is by far the largest island in the Seychelles, being 27km long and 8km wide. With granite peaks rising to 905m, tropical vegetation and magnificent beaches, Mahé also affords the greatest contrasts in scenery found anywhere in the archipelago.

Geography

The island divides roughly into two regions, the more rugged and hilly north and west, and the flatter and more gentle south and east. In the north are found the highest peaks – the Morne Seychellois (905m), the Trois Frères (699m) and the Morne Blanc (667m) – as well as the most densely populated and most touristically developed stretches of coastline. The 1.5km strip of white sand at Beau Vallon Bay, barely 10 minutes by car from the capital Victoria, is the largest and most popular beach on Mahé. In the few kilometres separating Danzilles and Glacis there are ten hotels and guest houses and facilities for almost all beach and watersports. In the south on the other hand, where the hills are at most only 500m high, extensive coconut and tropical fruit plantations and picturesque small villages dominate the scene.

On the east side around Victoria, and round most of the south of the island too, a relatively broad strip of level lowland borders the sea. The west coast by comparison is rugged, its hills and mountains often dropping steeply straight to the shore. This contrast is soon to become even more pronounced. Between the harbour and Pointe La Rue Airport, 124ha of new land have already been reclaimed from the lagoon inside the coral reef. This is the site earmarked for the sports stadia (athletics arena, swimming pools, gymnasia, tennis courts) and associated facilities for the "Indian Ocean Games", due to take place in 1993. It is on the west coast that the smaller, more secluded beaches are to be found – such as Anse Intendance, Anse Takamaka, Anse Gaulettes and Anse à la Mouche to the south, and Anse L'Islette further north. Mid-way up the west coast is Grand Anse, one of Mahé's longest beaches. From November to April huge waves make it ideal for surfing.

Luxuriant vegetation covers the entire island like a thick carpet, even in the suburbs of Victoria itself. Only on the steep slopes of the granite massifs

93

Mahé

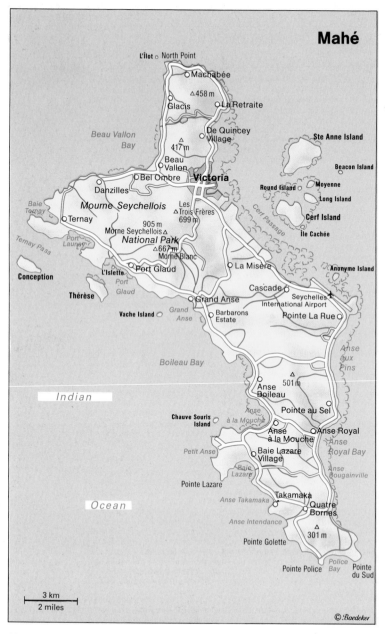

Mahé

L'Îlot ○ North Point

○ Machabée

△458 m

Glacis ○ ○ La Retraite

Beau Vallon Bay

De Quincey Village ○
△ 417 m

Beau Vallon ○

○ Bel Ombre **Victoria**

Danzilles ○

Ste Anne Island

Beacon Island

Round Island ○ **Moyenne**
Long Island

Cerf Island

Île Cachée

Cerf Passage

Mourne Seychellois

Les △ Trois Frères 699 m

Baie Ternay

Ternay ○

905 m
Morne Seychellois △

National Park

Port Launay

△667 m
Morne Blanc

Ternay Pass

L'Islette ○ ○ Port Glaud

○ La Misère

Anonyme Island

Port Glaud

Conception

Thérèse

Cascade ○

Seychelles International Airport ✈

Grand Anse ○

○ Barbarons Estate

Vache Island ○

Grand Anse

Pointe La Rue ○

Anse aux Pins

Boileau Bay

Indian

△ 501 m

Anse ○ Boileau

Chauve Souris Island

Anse à la Mouche

Pointe au Sel ○

Anse ○ à la Mouche ○ **Anse Royal**

Petit Anse

Baie Lazare ○ Village

Anse Royal Bay

Baie Lazare

Anse Bougainville

Pointe Lazare

Anse Takamaka

Takamaka ○ ○ **Quatre Borres**

Ocean

Anse Intendance

△ 301 m

Pointe Golette

Pointe Police *Police Bay* Pointe du Sud

3 km
2 miles

© *Baedeker*

94

Frangipane . . .

. . . and Wright Gardinia

does the grey, grey-brown or sometimes slightly reddish rock show through the green foliage. Thousands of years of erosion have left their distinctive traces on these rocks – evenly spaced vertical or slanting furrows which could almost have been carved by human hands.

Climate

As is the case with all the Seychelles islands Mahé's climate shows little variation throughout the year – though rainfall does tend to be somewhat above average from December to March and in the transitional months of April/May and October/November it may hardly rain at all. The north of the island experiences considerably more precipitation than the south, the approaching moist air being forced upwards by the hills. The mountain-tops in particular are often shrouded in cloud for days on end while the beaches below are bathed in glorious sunshine.

Calm conditions, perfect for diving and snorkelling, can always be found in the lee of the island, sheltered from the prevailing monsoon – i.e. on the north-west coast from June to September (European summer) and the south-east coast from December to March (European winter).

Origin of the island's name

On first discovering the island in 1742 Lazare Picault chose to call it Île d'Abondance – "Island of Plenty". On his second visit a couple of years later, however, he renamed it Mahé after Bertrand François Mahé de Labourdonnais, French Governor of the "Île de France" (now Mauritius) who had commissioned both expeditions,.

History

The first settlement was founded not on Mahé itself but on the tiny island of Ste Anne just off the coast, the earliest settlement on Mahé being at Anse Royal in 1771/72. In 1778 a garrison called "l'Établissement du Roi" was set up on the site of present day Victoria. This soon came to be known simply as "Établissement" or "Port Royal". In 1838 it was renamed "Port of Victoria" in honour of the British queen.

Population

Mahé is home to 88.5% of the inhabitants of the Seychelles, giving the island a population density of 400/sq.km. This population is very unevenly distributed, however. About 34,000 people live in the north (including Victoria) and about 19,000 in the south and south-east. Only about 6000 live in the highlands.

N.B.

While the Seychelles are blessed with a great and astonishingly varied and interesting natural beauty, they are less well endowed with historic buildings, art treasures and other such "sights". Because of this only the capital Victoria and Mahé's other main settlements are described in separate entries below. Further recommendations for sightseeing excursions by car are contained in the three routes suggested in the Facts annd Figures Section, Suggested Routes. Places on the island are described in clockwise order, beginning with Victoria.

Victoria

Altitude: 0–200m
Population: 23,000

Location and importance

Victoria, capital of the Republic of Seychelles, is situated in the north-east of the island of Mahé, in a bay protected from the open sea by the offshore islands of the Ste Anne group. Gaps in the fringing coral reef at this point enable larger ships to enter the natural harbour. The town itself extends along the narrow coastal strip from Pointe Conan in the north almost as far as Brillant Point in the south, as well as up the steep slopes of the hills behind.

Districts

There is no clear-cut line of demarcation between the urban area and population of Victoria and the rural communities surrounding it. Victoria

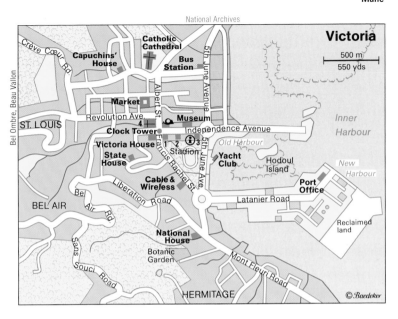

itself comprises a number of districts (population in brackets) including Mont Fleuri (*c.* 5100), Plaisance (*c.* 6600), Bel Air (*c.* 2400), St Louis (*c.* 3700), Mt Buxton (*c.* 3100) and part of English River (*c.* 2200). Victoria is one of the smallest capitals in the world and the only real town in the Seychelles. It is the administrative and economic centre of the Republic and possesses the only proper harbour.

Settlement of what is now Victoria began only in 1778, with the founding of a garrison known as "l'Établissement du Roi". Its troops were responsible for keeping the peace between the settlers on Ste Anne and those at Anse Royal.
Being conveniently located on the shores of the island's one natural harbour "Établissement" soon developed into its most important settlement.

History

In 1862 the only cyclone ever to strike the island devastated the town, killing about a hundred people. In 1903 Victoria became the capital of the newly independent British Crown Colony of the Seychelles, which up until then had been a dependency of Mauritius.

1971 saw the opening of the international airport at Pointe La Rue, about 10km south of the town. Since 1972 reclamation work has been in progress to the south of the old harbour. A total of 1.24sq.km have so far been recovered from the sea.

Description of the town

Victoria is an exceedingly busy little place on weekdays, but on Sundays hardly anyone or anything seems to stir. Town life revolves round two centres in particular: the clock tower at the intersection of Francis Rachel

General

Mahé

Street, Albert Street, Independence Avenue and State House Avenue, and the weekday market in old Market Street.

Clock tower

The silver coloured clock tower or "L'Horloge" was erected in 1903, when the Seychelles became an independent colony. It is a small replica of the tower at London's Vauxhall Bridge, not – as is often assumed – of the more famous Big Ben tower. At the time of its completion it was Victoria's tallest edifice and is now the town's real centre.

Around the clock tower cluster several banks, the main post office, "Victoria House" (a modern shopping precinct complete with arcade) and the colonial style law courts in front of which souvenir vendors display their wares. Right next to it, in the "Maison de l'Artisanat", craftwork typical of the island can be found on sale.

** National Museum

On the left a few metres along Independence Avenue, in the direction of the harbour, stands the Carnegie Building, built in 1911 with an endowment from the British-born steel magnate Andrew Carnegie. It houses the Seychelles National Museum where art exhibitions are also regularly held. Exhibits include documents illustrating the history of the Seychelles, and a model of Victoria in 1955 which highlights how great has been the town's expansion in the last 30 years. There are also displays of cultural and natural history with items such as the roof slab of a pirate's grave, the original "stone of possession" erected on Mahé by Nicolas Morphey in 1756, a pair of very beautiful and rare examples of cocos de mer, and various animal artefacts and specimens of coral. The 35cm statuette of Queen Victoria is thought to be the world's smallest of a ruling monarch. Also in the museum is an 1840 printing press on which the colony's first newspaper – "Le Seychellois" – was printed.

Opposite the museum is the "Pirates Arms", a café with a large terrace much frequented by those who want to see and be seen. The French

"Bicentennial" a sculpture by Lorenzo Appiani

98

Cultural Centre occupies part of the same building. Further along, beyond the National Bank and Independence House (government offices including the Seychelles Tourist Office), a large roundabout is the setting for a sculpture commemorating Victoria's bicentenary (1770–1970). The work of Lorenzo Appiani, a Seychellois artist of Italian extraction, its three wings symbolise Europe, Africa and Asia, the continents from which the various peoples of the Seychelles originally came.

From the roundabout a short detour leads to the old harbour. Here Hodoul Island is a reminder of the infamous corsair who ravaged merchant shipping in the Indian Ocean in the 18th c. His latter years were spent as a highly respected magistrate under the British, with whom he had previously warred.

Old harbour

Beyond the stadium and the yacht club, at the southern end of 5th June Avenue, is another roundabout also graced by a statue, very similar in fact to the first. This one was erected on the twelth anniversary of "liberation" (as President René's coup on June 5th 1977 is officially known). On the left can be seen the installations of the new port, constructed on land built up from the sea bed. It was officially opened by Britain's Princess Margaret.

New harbour

From the new harbour Francis Rachel Street leads back to the town centre past the Cable and Wireless building and the site of the new National Library (financed partly by donation). Although sadly no longer catering for guests the oldest hotel in the Seychelles, the "Hôtel de l'Equateur", continues to grace Poudrière Lane, a small side street directly behind Cable and Wireless.

Back at the clock tower a left turn and walk of about 200m along State House Avenue leads to State House (the governor's residence in colonial days). The house was designed in 1910 by a Mrs Davidson, wife of the then governor. It now serves as the presidential offices. In the grounds (not open

State House

View of the harbour of Victoria

Mahé

The Catholic Cathedral in Victoria

to the public) are the grave of Quéau de Quinssy, who died in 1827, and a bust of Pierre Poivres who established the first cinnamon and spice plantations on the island in 1772.

Sans Souci, Bel Air

Having again returned to the clock tower go along Albert Street, turning left at St Paul's Anglican Cathedral into Revolution Avenue. This runs perfectly straight for several hundred metres and leads to the hilly suburbs of St Louis, Bel Air and – via Sans Souci Road – Sans Souci. In 1956/57 Archbishop Makarios of Cyprus spent his exile in the villa in Sans Souci now occupied by the US embassy. The cemetery at Bel Air contains the graves of the pirate Jean François Hodoul and a certain Pierre Louis Poiret who, before his death in 1856, claimed to be Louis XVII, son of Louis XVI and Marie Antoinette.

*Grand Trianon

Just at the point where Revolution Avenue bends for the first time can be seen one of the finest examples of colonial architecture in the Seychelles, "Grand Trianon". It was here that the explorer Henry Morton Stanley stayed after searching for David Livingstone in Africa. The house is now a restaurant.

Market

On the way back to the town centre a left turn into either Quincey Street or Benezet Street leads to the Sir Selwyn Clarke Market, some 200m further on. The market is one of the most colourful and popular places in Victoria. It is named after the governor who, in the 1940s, contributed much to the cause of public education in the islands. For this he was reviled by the wealthier settlers as a "socialist". Fish, spices, vegetables and tropical fruit are all brought here for sale. It is a meeting place for virtually the whole island, especially on Saturdays between 5 and 8 o'clock in the morning. In the streets around the market there are some good examples of traditional Seychelles colonial architecture.

Catholic Cathedral

Just a little way beyond the market, at the far end of Church Street, stands the Roman Catholic Cathedral of the Immaculate Conception, completed in

1874. Here children born in wedlock are christened on Sundays, and those born out of wedlock – who considerably outnumber them – are christened on Fridays. The chimes of "Le Clocher" (the cathedral clock tower, built in 1936) sound the hour twice, once at the correct time and again a few minutes later, as if to rouse the tardy and the lie-a-beds. "Le Clocher" now has its own small place in the world's literature, featuring in the novel "Where the Clocks Chime Twice" by the English writer Alec Waugh. Like the clock tower, the Capuchin friary next door to the cathedral was built in the thirties.

Valuable documents relating to the geography, history and literature of the Seychelles are stored in the National Archives, reached by following the English River road or the coast road northwards.

National Archives

In the opposite direction on the south side of the town, to the right at the top end of Mont Fleuri Road (the airport road), are the Botanic Gardens. They were laid out in 1901, modelled on the famous Curepipe Gardens (collection of tropical plants) in Mauritius. There are only a limited number of native plants in this delightful and beautifully kept park, however – a handful of coco de mer palms, bread-fruit trees and "lataniers". The remainder (95%) of the plants are imported varieties referred to by the Seychellois as "exotic". One or two animals native to the Seychelles can also be seen in this tranquil setting, including giant tortoises and flying foxes.

Botanic Gardens

Adjoining the Botanic Gardens is the Bel Air orchid garden. After a lengthy confrontation the garden was compulsorily acquired from its former owner, who subsequently set fire to large parts of the valuable plant collection.

Coastal waters near Cascade

Cascade

	Altitude: sea level Population: (district) 2300 Distance from Victoria: 8km
St Andrew's Church	Cascade is a small village on the road from Victoria to the airport. Its church, dedicated to St Andrew, is enthroned on a rock pedestal and is visible from far and wide. There is a saint's day procession to the church on 30th November when the villagers' boats are also blessed.
Path to the waterfall	From the little lagoon directly below the church a footpath cuts inland into the hills. After a climb of about 30 or 40 minutes it ends at the Cascade River waterfall from which the village takes its name.

Anse Royal

	Altitude: sea level Population: (district): 4200 Distance from Victoria: 20km
General	Anse Royal, in the bay of that name, is Mahé's oldest settlement. It was founded by Gillot in 1771/72 on the instructions of Pierre Poivre and is now the island's second largest centre. Gillot's brief was to establish the "Jardin du Roi" plantation, where Poivre successfully introduced the first cinnamon trees and other spice plants. Worth seeing here are two churches, one built in 1889, the other in 1930.
Anse Royal bay	The long beach at Anse Royal bay is a favourite with the inhabitants of Mahé. Snorkellers in particular will find the lagoon to their liking, sheltered as it is by the fringing reef. A number of guest houses and restaurants are located along this particular stretch of coast.

Baie Lazare village

	Altitude: 50–100m Population: (district) 2200 Distance from Victoria: 26km
General	Dominating the village and affording a pleasant view over the bay is the neo-Gothic church of St Francis of Assisi. Both Baie Lazare bay and village were named after Lazare Picault, commander of the French expedition which, in 1742, first set foot on Seychelles soil.
Baie Lazare	It is only a short walk from Baie Lazare village to Val Mer and Baie Lazare beach, likewise to the beaches at Anse Soleil and Anse la Liberté. Anse Soleil and its little settlement are privately owned and the inhabitants sometimes levy a "toll" on anyone visiting the beach.
Plantation	Inland from Baie Lazare is Val d'Endor, the largest tropical fruit plantation in the Seychelles.

Anse à la Mouche

	Altitude: sea level Population: (district Anse Louis): 1450 Distance from Victoria: 22km
General	Anse à la Mouche was one of the earliest settlements in the Seychelles. Its colonial houses, some as much as 150 years old, are widely scattered and

often lie hidden among the trees. One of these houses – situated at the point where Anse à la Mouche becomes Anse aux Poules Bleues, on the main road north from Baie Lazare village – has been turned into a studio and gallery home by the artist Michael Adams.

Unlike other beaches on Mahé's west coast this one enjoys the shelter of a fringing reef and is safe for bathing even in windy weather. In the afternoons fishing boats returning with their catch provide an interesting diversion (as they also do at Anse Boileau village just to the north). Their fishing trips sometimes last several days and take them to the more remote outlying islands.

The beach

Grand Anse

Altitude: sea level
Population: (district): 1850
Distance from Victoria: 12km

Grand Anse boasts one of Mahé's longest and most attractive sandy beaches, unfortunately made dangerous for bathing by strong currents (in 1962 the then Governor of the Seychelles was drowned here). Located one at each end of Grand Anse are two large hotels, the Barbarons Beach and the Equator.
Intensive use has been made of the narrow coastal strip at Grand Anse. In addition to a government-owned model farm it is also the site of a major satellite tracking station, the aerial masts of which can be seen from afar.

Grand Anse

Port Glaud

Altitude: sea level
Population (district): 1400
Distance from Victoria: 12km

Port Glaud is Mahé's second most important tourist centre after Beau Vallon, popular despite a lack of beaches on this particular stretch of coast. Holidaymakers who stay in the hotels here take advantage of the excellent bathing and watersports on the nearby island of Thérèse (see entry).

Tourist centre

Spread across the slopes of Morne Blanc above Port Glaud are the largest tea plantations on Mahé. Their produce can be sampled at a pleasant tea-room on the Forêt Noire road, from which a delightful view is gained of the coast and the islands dotted along it.

Tea plantations

On the hillside a kilometre or so inland stands Mission Lodge, an Anglican mission school which was opened in 1875 (only to close in 1889). Huge sandragon trees line the short avenue from the road and also the parking place leading to another fine vantage point.

Mission Lodge

North of Port Glaud, the headland known as Pointe l'Escalier (separating Anse l'Islette from Port Launay) has a feature of particular interest. When viewed from the seaward side a series of strange, regular steps are seen, giving the distinct impression of having been hewn out of the rock. It remains unclear as to whether this "staircase" is natural or whether it was the work of the Malayan peoples who stopped here on their voyages to Madagascar.

Pointe l'Escalier

Bel Ombre

Altitude: sea level
Population (district): 1900
Distance from Victoria: 6km

Mahé

General

Bel Ombre's long but narrow stretch of sand may not be as lovely as the neighbouring beach at Beau Vallon but it has the advantage of being much less crowded – especially at weekends. Bel Ombre can also boast two or three of the best restaurants on Mahé, as well as the hotel catering school which runs its own restaurant serving midday meals.

Excavations

The cliffs at the western end of the beach still bear marks of the excavations carried out some years ago (backed by seemingly limitless resources) in a vain search for the treasure thought to have been buried there by the legendary pirate La Buse. Before being hanged on the island of Réunion La Buse is reputed to have thrown a coded message into the crowd, a clue to the whereabouts of his priceless hoard. In so doing he whetted the appetites of generations of treasure seekers.

Beau Vallon

Altitude: sea level
Population (district): 3500
Distance from Victoria: 4km

Beau Vallon Bay

The beach at Beau Vallon is the most popular bathing beach on the island. It is also one of the longest (*c.* 1.5km) and widest (20 to 25m) palm-shaded beaches in the Seychelles. It extends along the shores of Beau Vallon Bay where 33% of Mahé's tourist facilities are concentrated. Here, particularly in the vicinity of the resort's two largest hotels, a great variety of beach activities and watersports are catered for.

Entertainment

Beau Vallon's hotels also provide the liveliest nightlife of anywhere in the Seychelles, with dance evenings and folk displays enjoyed by tourists and islanders alike. Only foreigners patronise the casino, however, entry being barred to the Seychellois.

The beach at Beau Vallon Bay

From Beau Vallon Bay there are boat trips to the islands of Thérèse and Conception on the west coast and to the large island of Silhouette further off to the north-west.

Boat trips

Marianne

Area: 0.95sq.km
Population: between 5 and 10

Boats to Marianne from Praslin and La Digue.

Getting there

Marianne (4°21'S 55°55'E) is one of the islands in the Praslin group. It is situated 4km south-east of Félicité, 8km east of La Digue and 58km north-east of Mahé (see entries).

Location and general

This small granite island on the eastern edge of the Mahé Plateau rises to a height of 128m above sea level. Its only inhabitants are the manager and workers on the coconut plantation .

Moyenne – Île Moyenne

Area: 0.09sq.km
Population: 8

The crossing by boat from Victoria takes 10 minutes. A single guest house, a small restaurant and a kiosk cater for visitors.

Getting there

Moyenne, privately owned, lies sandwiched between the islands of Ste Anne and Cerf (see entries) in the Sainte Anne Marine National Park. It is 5km off Victoria and only a few hundred metres north of Long Island (see entry).

Location and general

Visitors are welcome on the tiny (450m by 250m) island with its numerous tropical plants (among which are takamaka trees and casuarinas).

Lazare Picault christened the island "Moyenne" in 1742 on account of its position between three others, Ste Anne, Long Island and Round Island. Two hundred years ago it was a pirate's lair and treasure is once again supposed to be buried here waiting to be unearthed. From 1899 to 1919 an Englishwoman kept a dogs' home on the island for Mahé's strays (the ruins of which can still be seen).

History

A marked trail runs round the island; some of the trees are labelled.

Trail

The island's cemetery, mentioned in documents dating as far back as 1892, has only two graves both of which are presumed to be of pirates.

Item of interest

Moyenne's British owner Brendan Grimshaw greatly enjoys recounting tales of ghosts and pirates – all taking place on his island of course.

North Island – Île du Nord

Area: 2.01sq.km
Population: 80

Boats from Mahé (Port Glaud, Beau Vallon Bay) take day-trippers to North Island from time to time.

Getting there

North Island (4°23'S 55°15'E) is situated 30km north-west of Mahé and 6km north of Silhouette.

Location and general

Plate – Île Plate

North, typical of the granite islands of the Mahé Plateau, was one of the first in the Seychelles to be explored by the British (in 1609). Only 2sq.km in area it nevertheless rises 214m above sea level and has only a modest amount of cultivated land. The islanders' houses are arranged in a long row by the beach.

Plate – Île Plate

Area: 0.54sq.km
Inhabitants: none

Location

Plate (5°50'S 55°20'E) lies 140km south of Mahé. Like Coëtivy it is an isolated coral island, standing apart from any island group.

Poivre (Atoll)

See Amirantes – Les Amirantes, African Banks, St Joseph (Atoll), Poivre (Atoll)

Praslin

Area: 37.56sq.km
Population: 4800
Principal settlement: Baie Ste Anne

Flights

Praslin is linked to Mahé by a regular air service with up to twenty flights a day. The journey by Air Seychelles' Twin Otter and Britten-Norman Islander aircraft takes only 15 to 20 minutes.

By boat

The crossing (e.g. by the "Arctic Tern", "La Belle Praslinoise" or "La Bellone") takes about 2½ hours.

Accommodation

Praslin has a total of 300 tourist beds in three large and ten smaller hotels, guest houses and pensions. After Mahé it is by far the most popular holiday destination in the Seychelles.

Leisure and sport

Sport and entertainment are less varied than on Mahé but still offer plenty of options including windsurfing, diving and snorkelling, big game fishing, cycling, walking and waterskiing. Conditions for snorkelling and diving are particularly good in the waters around the small island of St Pierre and around Curieuse (see entry), also at Anse Petite Cour and Anse Possession on the north-east coast and Anse La Blague in the south-east

Location

Praslin is situated between 4°17' and 4°22'S, 55°41' and 55°48'E. It is 38km from Mahé, 5km from La Digue, 10km from Aride and 15km from Félicité. The island is 12km long, 5km across at its widest point, and roughly north-west–south-east in orientation.

Climate

Praslin's climate is very similar to Mahé's – though being lower it has less rainfall and lacks the latter's high altitude cloud zones. The water supply comes from the biggest of the island's waterfalls, in the Vallée de Mai.

History and origin of the name

Lazare Picault discovered the island in 1744 on his second voyage of discovery to the Seychelles. Because of the dense covering of coco de mer palms he called it "Île aux Palmes". Later, when Marion Dufresne took official possession of the island for France in 1768 it was renamed in honour of Gabriel de Choiseul, Duke of Praslin and French Minister of Marine.

Baie Ste Anne, the chief place on Praslin

Coastal villages and bays

Praslin is the second largest granite island in the Seychelles archipelago. It consists of several ranges of hills the highest summit of which reaches 367m above sea level. It is considerably less mountainous in character than Mahé, the red granite being moulded into gentle hills rather than precipitous rock faces. The beaches on Praslin are even more attractive and longer than those on Mahé, especially the ones on the east coast and at Anse Lazio in the north.

Baie Ste Anne is the principal settlement on the island; the main hospital, the biggest school, the landing pier, a bank, post office and police station all being located here. The coast road running north from the village forks after less than 2km kilometres. The right-hand branch goes to Anse La Blague, a bay which, while not a particular beauty spot, offers some of the best diving on Praslin. An artist has his home at Petite Anse.

Baie Ste Anne

The left-hand fork cuts through the palm groves towards Côte d'Or and Anse Volbert, a long, wide stretch of sand bounded in the south by Anse Gouvernement with its newly built (and by Seychelles standards rather luxurious) hotel, and in the north – beyond Pointe Zanguilles – by Anse Petite Cour.

Anse Volbert

Anse Possession, just a few hundred metres further north again, is the bay where in 1768 Marion Dufresne laid official claim to the island for France, erecting a "stone of possession" and giving Praslin its present name (it had been known until then as "Île aux Palmes", see p. 106).

Anse Possession

A little further on at Anse Boudin the road turns inland and then branches again. The left fork leads to a transmitting station in the hills, the right to Anse Lazio, the prettiest beach on Praslin and one of the most delightful anywhere in the Seychelles. During the north-west monsoon high, crystal-

**Anse Lazio

107

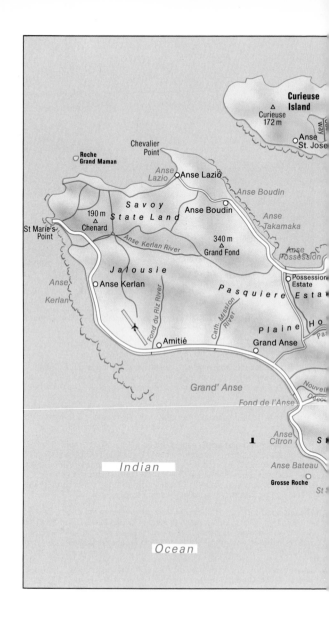

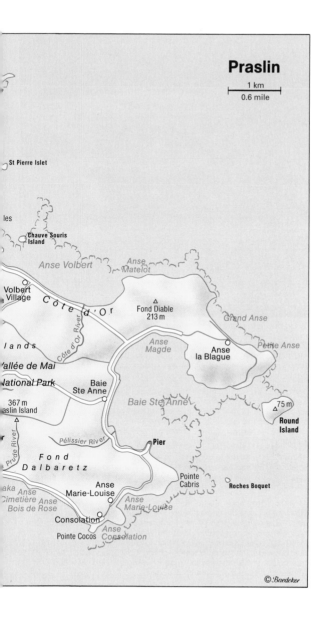

Praslin

1 km
0.6 mile

St Pierre Islet

les

Chauve Souris
Island

Anse Volbert

*Anse
Matelot*

Volbert
Village

Côte d'Or

Fond Diable
213 m

Grand Anse

Côte d'Or River

l a n d s

*Anse
Magde*

Anse
la Blague

Petite Anse

*Vallée de Mai
National Park*

Baie
Ste Anne

Baie Ste Anne

367 m
aslin Island

75 m

Round
Island

Pélissier River

Pier

Pr de River

F o n d
D a l b a r e t z

Pointe
Cabris

Roches Boquet

aka *Anse
Cimetière*
*Anse
Bois de Rose*

Anse
Marie-Louise

*Anse
Marie-Louise*

Consolation

Pointe Cocos

*Anse
Consolation*

© *Baedeker*

The beautiful Anse Lazio bay in the north of the island

clear waves break on its undulating shoreline and over the smooth-worn red granite boulders scattered like great marbles in the sea. In recent years Anse Lazio has become much better known and many more people now frequent this once rather secluded spot.

Pointe Cabris

The road to the landing pier at Baie Ste Anne runs past the large school, the Catholic church and a small boatyard. Just before the parking place at the harbour mole it branches right, climbing the headland of Pointe Cabris in steep zigzags to the little "Château de Feuilles" hotel, widely acknowledged to be the gastronomic Mecca of the islands because of its excellent cuisine.

Anse Consolation

Beyond the hotel the road continues to Anse Marie-Louise and Anse Consolation at the southern tip of Praslin. Anse Consolation has an interesting although not particularly beautiful beach, with strange rock and coral formations. From here Mahé is clearly visible in good weather.

Grand Anse

At Anse Consolation the asphalt road becomes a well-used sand track which runs along the narrow sandy beach the entire length of the island's south-east coast to Grand Anse. For anyone in search of a meal there is a recently opened restaurant along the way, facing the little rocky islet of "Grande Roche" (there is also a beach for swimming).
Just before Grand Anse (Praslin's second most important settlement) the track joins up with the asphalt road from the Vallée de Mai and Baie Ste Anne which comes out here on the coast.

Northwards the coastal strip begins to open out and in places becomes almost park-like with plantations bordering the road. Three smallish hotels cater for holidaymakers who prefer to escape the tourist bustle of Anse Volbert. Further on still Praslin's small airport comes into view on the right.

St Marie's Point

Towards the island's northern end the beaches also widen out again. The road curves inland to avoid the large poultry farm and then divides. To the

St Marie's Point

left a narrow track leads back to the beach at Anse Kerlan, and on to the spectacular cliffs of St Marie's Point from where there is a marvellous view of the headland's twin crescent-shaped beaches, situated back to back and separated only by the narrowest tongue of land. Forking right the white cement road climbs steeply up through woods, ending after a few hundred metres at a little settlement. From here there is a footpath to Anse Lazio.

**Vallée de Mai National Park

In the centre of the island, towards its southern end, is the Vallée de Mai National Park. This unique valley – home of the legendary coco de mer – enables the visitor to get an idea of the vegetation existing on the island prior to the arrival of Europeans.

Figures in brackets refer to the plan (p. 113) of Vallée de Mai nature trail.   **N.B.**

Adorning the entrance to the National Park are several 20 to 30m high coco de mer palms, both "male" and "female". Being well spaced out the dangling seed and fruit panicles are clearly visible. A thick forest of coco de mer and latanier palms clothes the floor of the valley and the lower slopes, so dense in places that the sun's rays hardly penetrate. Growing on the drier north-west facing hills are palmiste palms and other native species of timber.

Close to the park entrance (1) the vegetation is still mixed. In addition to "bois rouge" (redwoods), philodendrons are much in evidence. These latter, familiar in Europe, are troublesome intruders in this environment, capable of posing a real threat to the endemic palms.

Assuming a growth rate of about 5cm per annum for young trees (even less for older ones), the thick stand of coco de mer palms a few metres along on the right (2) has probably been there for more than a thousand years. Such

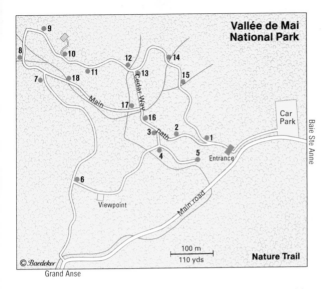

dense tracts constitute small, closed bio-systems, the resilience of which probably saved the coco de mer palm from extinction in the face of largely catastrophic settlement by Europeans.

Turn left where the path next branches (3) and go down into one of the loveliest groves of mixed palms in the Seychelles (4). Near to the course of the little stream the trees grow even closer together (5), among them being five of the Seychelles' six endemic palm species (including three latanier palms) and three of the four endemic "vacoas" or screw pines.

Returning along the same path to (4) bear left towards a viewing lodge on higher ground. From this vantage point the various different vegetation zones in the valley are clearly identifiable.

A few hundred metres further on (6) the path threads its way (7) through another dense coco de mer grove. There are trees of all ages, with one or two palmiste palms growing amongst them. A short distance beyond is a bench (8) from where the tallest of all the Vallée de Mai's coco der mer palms (over 30m) is visible straight up the slope opposite. The path continues uphill (9) and, after a short detour to another viewpoint, arrives at a grove (10) consisting almost entirely of "bois rouge" – an example of the vegetation typical of middle altitudes in the pre-colonial period.

Next comes another stand of redwoods (11) on the far side of which is a bridge (12). The stream it crosses springs from the rocks a short distance away. In the evenings this is a good place to see one of the species of gecko (*Aeluronyx Seychellensis*) endemic to the Seychelles.

Almost immediately (13) the path forks. Cedar Walk branches off to the right, soon joining up again with the main path through the park (16). The other fork leads to a bridge (14) over an often dry watercourse and on to yet another bridge (15) from where it is only a short distance back to the start of the walk and the park entrance.

◀ *In Valèe de Mai National Park*

Turn down Cedar Walk and follow it southwards to the pond (16), known as "the lily pond" despite the complete absence of water-lilies. Striking green tree frogs (*Megalixalus Seychellensis*) frequent the pond at night. Above the lily pond the main path (left at the intersection) makes its way northwards through the park. Set amidst the tropical vegetation are two more bridges (17), (18).

Black parrots

The black parrots are another attraction of the Vallée de Mai National Park. These birds spend most of their time feeding on fruit-bearing trees but they can also often be seen in the vicinity the kiosk at the car park or at the park entrance.

Providence (Atoll)

See Farquhar (Atoll), St Pierre, Providence (Atoll)

Round Island – Île Ronde

Area: 0.02sq.km
Inhabitants: 1

Getting there

Boat trips – some in glass bottomed boats – run to Round Island from Mahé.

Location and general

Round Island, barely 200m across, is part of the Sainte Anne Marine National Park. It lies in the bay of Victoria, about 4km off the coast of Mahé and 0.9km from Ste Anne. The tiny island – not to be confused with the island of the same name south-east of Praslin – was discovered by Lazare Picault in 1742 and christened "Île Ronde" (Round Island) because of its shape.

In the 19th c. there was a women's leper colony on the island. Today the Sainte Anne Marine National Park is managed from here.

Ste Anne Island

Area: 2.19sq.km
Inhabitants: employees of the National Youth Service camp

Location and general

Ste Anne Island (Sainte Anne) is the most northerly island in the Sainte Anne Marine National Park and lies about 5km from the harbour at Victoria. At 2.2km long and 1.4km wide it is the largest of the group of islands in the bay of Victoria to which it has given its name. The top of Mount Ste Anne, the highest point, is 250m above sea level. Because of the presence of a National Youth Service camp special permission is required to visit the island.

History and origin of the name

Lazare Picault discovered the island – together with Mahé – on St Anne's Day 1742, naming it after the saint. In 1770 the first permanent European settlement in the Seychelles was set up here, abandoned not long afterwards in favour of a new site on Mahé.

*Sainte Anne Marine National Park

The National Park to which the island gave its name was established by the Seychelles government in 1973. It includes the rest of the islands in the group – Cerf Island, Long Island, Moyenne, Round Island (see entries) – as well as the surrounding coral banks. Fishing and the collection of coral, shells and live shellfish and snails are all banned. There are some good places for diving, especially off the south coast of Ste Anne. Oil storage

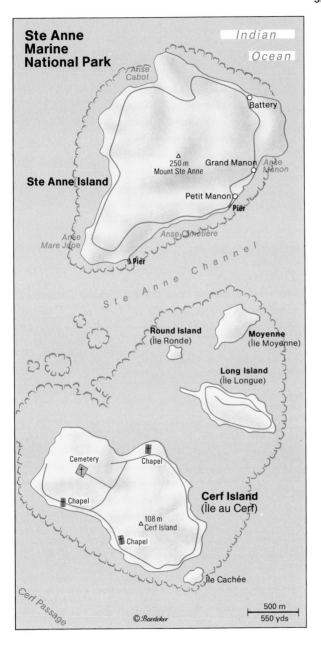

Ste Anne Marine National Park

Indian

Ocean

Anse Cabot

Battery

Ste Anne Island

△ 250 m Mount Ste Anne

Grand Manon

Anse Manon

Petit Manon

Pier

Anse Mare Jupe

Pier

Anse Cimetière

Ste Anne Channel

Round Island (Île Ronde)

Moyenne (Île Moyenne)

Long Island (Île Longue)

Cemetery

Chapel

Chapel

Cerf Island (Île au Cerf)

△ 108 m Cerf Island

Chapel

Île Cachée

Cerf Passage

© *Baedeker*

500 m
550 yds

Bird's eye view of Ste Anne Island

tanks erected on the island in the late seventies greatly detract from the otherwise natural harmony.

Sainte Anne Marine National Park

See Cerf Island
See Long Island
See Moyenne
See Round Island
See Ste Anne Island

St François (Atoll)

See Alphonse, Bijoutier, St François (Atoll)

St Joseph (Atoll)

See Amirantes – Les Amirantes, African Banks, St Joseph (Atoll), Poivre (Atoll)

St Pierre

See Farquhar (Atoll), St Pierre, Providence (Atoll)

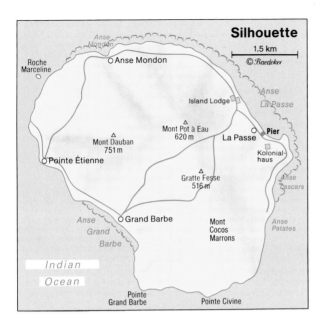

Palms on a beach of Silhouette

Silhouette

Area: 19.95sq.km
Population: *c.* 200

Getting there	The crossing by boat from Mahé takes about 1 hour.
Leisure and sport	Silhouette's beaches are perfect for bathing and snorkelling. Two bays on the south-east side, Anse Lascars and Anse Patates, are well-known for the pretty shells to be found there.
Location and general	Silhouette (4°30'S 55°15'E) lies 20km off the north-west coast of Mahé and 7km south of North Island.

From the point of view of its hilly topography, its flora and its fauna Silhouette, the third largest island in the archipelago, might almost be Mahé all over again. Despite being only 5.5km long and roughly the same in width it is capped by Mont Dauban (751m), second highest peak in the Seychelles. Part of the island is covered by dense virgin forest, an outstanding example of pre-colonial vegetation now so rare on Mahé. Carnivorous plants are also found there.

Settlements	There are small settlements at Anse Mondon in the north, Grand Barbe in the west and La Passe on the east coast (where Silhouette's only hotel and hospital are located). The island has no roads, just tracks. It is quite big enough to get lost on and walkers should if possible take a guide.
Economy	Silhouette's inhabitants make their living almost exclusively from copra. In addition there are one or two fairly small cinnamon plantations and sugar cane, tropical fruit and vegetables, coffee and tobacco are also grown.
History and origin of the name	Graves on the island indicate that Arab seafarers called here at least occasionally as early as the 9th c. – at about the time of their discovery of

Sunset over Thérèse

the Comoros Islands. It is questionable, however, whether any real settlements were started.

The first European exploration of the island was in 1767 and in 1771 it was named after Etienne de Silhouette, Louis XV's "Contrôleur Général des Finances" and former Minister of Finance. He was the Frenchman whose plans for rescuing the royal finances were never presented in anything but the vaguest outline, as a result of which his name become enshrined in the language.

Sights

Among the most interesting things to see on Silhouette are the magnificent mausoleum of the Dauban family, proprietors of the island for many years; the old colonial house – one of the most attractive in the Seychelles – which now doubles as the island's only restaurant; and the thirty or so Arab graves at Anse Lascar. In addition the old sugar mill and the oil mill can also be visited.

Thérèse – Île Thérèse

Area: 0.74sq.km
Inhabitants: 2

There is a regular ferry service to the island from Port Glaud (Mahé). The crossing takes only a few minutes.

Getting there

Thérèse's delightful beaches are used chiefly by holidaymakers staying at hotels between Port Glaud and Grand Anse on Mahé (that stretch of coast having virtually no beaches).

Beaches

Thérèse is situated only 0.6km off the north-west coast of Mahé, sheltering the bay at Port Glaud from the open sea. The privately owned island is about 1.5km long, 0.75km wide and 164m above sea level at its highest point. There are still quite a number of giant tortoises living wild on the island.

Location and general

Practical Information

Where an address has more than one telephone number these are separated by a stroke. International and local dialling codes are given in brackets. **N.B.**

Airlines

Air Seychelles
Victoria House
Francis Rachel Street/
State House Avenue
P.O. Box 386
Victoria/Mahé
Tel. 25220; Fax. 25159;
Telex 2289 AIRFIN SZ

Air Travel

See entry — Getting to the Seychelles

There are airports or airstrips on the following islands: Mahé, Praslin, Frégate, Bird, Desroches, Denis, D'Arros, Marie Louise, Rémire, Alphonse, Astove, Farquhar and Coëtivy. — Airports

Air Seychelles (see Airlines) maintains a daily service to Praslin using nine-seater Britten-Norman Islanders and twenty-seater Twin Otters. It also runs the charter flights to Denis, Frégate, Desroches and Bird arranged by the hotels on those islands. — Air Seychelles

Information about other island flights can be obtained from:
Island Development Company
P.O. Box 638
New Port/Victoria. Tel. 24640 — Information

Further information:
Seychelles International Airport (Pointe La Rue/Mahé): tel. 76501
International flights and air freight: tel. 73051
Inland flights: tel. 73101;
Praslin Airport: tel. 33214

International reservations (Victoria House/Mahé): tel. 73101; telex 2337 AIRSEY SZ
Inland reservations (Seychelles International Airport/Mahé): tel. 73101; telex 2314 AIRSEY SZ;
Praslin Airport: tel. 33214 — Reservations (Air Seychelles)

Schedule of inland flights:
Mahé – Praslin: up to 20 flights daily in each direction; duration 15 minutes.
Mahé – Frégate: twice daily (outward 0945 and 1625; return 1015 and 1650); duration 20 minutes.
Mahé – Bird: once daily (outward 1030; return 1120); duration 30–40 minutes. — Inland flights

◀ *The motorboat "La Créole"*

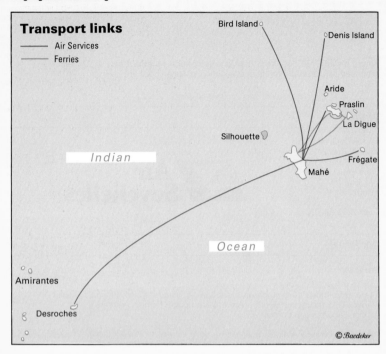

Transport links

— Air Services

— Ferries

Bird Island

Denis Island

Aride

Praslin

La Digue

Silhouette

Indian

Frégate

Mahé

Ocean

Amirantes

Desroches

© *Baedeker*

Mahé – Denis: thrice weekly (outward Wed. and Sun. 1400, Fri. 1100; return Wed. and Sun. 1450, Fri. 1150); duration 30–40 minutes.
Mahé – Desroches: thrice weekly (outward Mon., Wed. and Sat. 1300; return 1420); duration 1 hour.

Island hopping   See Excursions and Tour Operators

Angling and Sea Fishing

See Sport

Arts and Crafts

See Souvenirs

Banks

Business hours   Except where stated otherwise banks in the Seychelles open at the following times:
Mon.–Fri. 8.30 or 9am–1pm, 2 or 2.30–4 or 4.30pm. Some banks also open
on Sat. from 8.30 or 9am–noon.

A Boeing 767 of Air Seychelles

Banque Française Commerciale Océan Indien   Mahé
State House Avenue/Albert Street
P.O. Box 122
Victoria
Tel. 23096; Telex 2261 BAFROI SZ; Fax. 22676;
Anse Royal. Tel. 71166

Bank of Baroda/Labank Baroda
Albert Street
P.O. Box 124
Victoria
Tel. 23038/21533; Telex 2241 BARODA SZ

Bank of Credit and Commerce
Victoria House
Francis Rachel Street/State House Avenue
P.O. Box 579
Victoria
Tel. 22303/22305; Telex 2262 BCCI SZ; Fax. 21909
Counter at Pointe La Rue Airport
Business hours: Mon.–Fri. 9am–noon; also opens for international flights
(Eurocheques and traveller's cheques not accepted)

Barclays Bank International
Independence Avenue
P.O. Box 167
Victoria
Tel. 24101; Telex 2225 BARDCO SZ; Fax. 24678;
Victoria
Albert Street/Huteau Street
Tel. 24101; Telex 2308 BARMAR SZ;

Beau Vallon
Tel. 47391
Counter at Pointe La Rue Airport
Business hours: Mon.–Fri. 8.30am–12.30pm, Sat. 8.30–10.45am

Development Bank of Seychelles
Independence Avenue
P.O. Box 271
Victoria
Tel. 24471; Telex 2348 DEVBAN SZ; Fax. 24274

Habib Bank
Francis Rachel Street
P.O. Box 702
Victoria
Tel. 24371/2; Telex 2242 HABANK SZ

Seychelles Savings Bank
Independence Avenue
P.O. Box 531
Victoria. Tel. 25251

Standard Chartered Bank Africa PLC
Kingsgate House
Independence Avenue
P.O. Box 241
Victoria
Tel. 25011; Telex 2253 SCBSEY SZ; Fax. 24670

Praslin

Barclays Bank International
Grand Anse
Tel. 33344
Business hours: Mon.–Fri. 2.30–5.30pm;
Baie Ste Anne
Tel. 32218
Business hours: Mon.–Fri. 8.30am–noon

La Digue

Barclays Bank International
La Réunion
Tel. 34348
Business hours: Tues. and Thur. 11.30am–2pm

Seychelles Savings Bank
La Passe
Tel. 34335
Business hours: Mon.–Fri. 8.15am–1pm and 2–3.30pm

Beaches

General

There are many fascinating beaches in the Seychelles but only a few are really suitable for bathing. Dangerous currents can make swimming hazardous when a heavy swell sets into bays unprotected by a reef. Great care is needed and signs prohibiting bathing should be strictly observed.

Many beaches are plagued by beach fleas the bites of which can produce an allergic reaction in anyone susceptible. These insects are not really fleas but a type of mosquito which lives on the sand at certain times of the year. Insect repellents are normally sufficient protection.

The most effective precaution is to lie on a towel or mattress rather than directly on the sand.

Beware also of sea urchins and stone fish! Anyone unfortunate enough to be stung by the latter should seek immediate medical attention. Bathing or beach shoes should always be worn when reef walking in shallow water. There are relatively few jelly fish in the Seychelles but they can cause painful stings and poisoning. As protection against severe sunburn snorkellers should wear a T-shirt.

Mahé, the principal island in the Seychelles, has a total of 68 beaches. Most are small, the longest being a mere 3km. The chief and most attractive beaches are:

Beau Vallon Bay, the most popular beach of all. There are three large hotels and facilities for every kind of watersport.

Beaches on Mahé

Grand Anse, with its 2km long beach but no hotels. From November to April the very high waves sweeping into the bay making it excellent for surfing.

Anse à la Mouche which, unlike other beaches on the south-west side, offers safe swimming even in windy weather (being protected by a coral reef offshore).

Baie Lazare, with good snorkelling.

Anse Takamaka and Anse Intendance, among the most beautiful beaches on Mahé but dangerous for bathing.

Anse Royal Bay, where the beach – stretching for 3km – is one of the island's longest. The lagoon inside the reef is good for snorkelling but not particularly attractive for ordinary bathing.

On the west side of the island the beaches are kilometres-long but narrow and not very suitable for bathing. They extend from Anse Kerlan in the north-west to Pointe Cocos in the south and include Grand Anse, Anse Bateau and Anse Takamaka. They are deserted most of the time.

Beaches on Praslin

Paragliding on the beach of Beau Vallon Bay (Mahé)

The east coast has much more to offer, particularly the lovely wide beach at Anse Volbert, around which most of the island's hotels and facilities for sport and entertainment are concentrated. Also worth visiting is the delightful and lonely Anse Matelot, only 15 minutes away from the Hotel L'Archipel.

Anse Lazio in north Praslin must be one of the finest granite beaches anywhere in the Seychelles.

Beaches on La Digue

Anse La Réunion is both the longest beach on La Digue and well protected by a coral reef. Anse Patates on the other hand (at the island's northern end) is very exposed; big waves often break against its picturesque red granite rocks. Anse Gaulettes, Anse Grosse Roche and Anse Banane are much more suitable for bathing and snorkelling, the water being relatively shallow.

The island's three most striking beaches are all found on the south-east side, at Grand Anse, Petite Anse and Anse Cocos. There is no sheltering coral reef on this part of the coast however, and all are made dangerous by heavy swell during the south-east monsoon. There is another fine beach at Anse la Source à Jean (on the west coast, close to President France Albert René's weekend retreat at Union Estate) where distinctive rock formations jut out into the sea.

Bicycle Rental

See Car and Bicycle Rental

Boat Services

Getting there

See entry

General

Regular boat and ferry services link the islands of Mahé, Praslin and La Digue. There are also some passenger facilities aboard supply ships such as the "Cinq Juin" which call from time to time at the outlying islands. The return passage by sea to islands in the Amirantes group takes 12 days, to Farquhar and Aldabra 20 days.

Ferries

Ferry services to Praslin and La Digue (subject to change):

The "Arctic Tern": Mon., Wed. and Fri.; departs Victoria 7am, arrives Praslin 9am; departs Praslin noon, arrives La Digue 12.20pm; departs La Digue 3.30pm, arrives Mahé 5.45pm.

The "La Belle Praslinoise": Mon., Wed. and Fri.; departs Praslin (Baie Ste Anne) 5.30am, arrives Mahé 8.30am; departs Mahé 11am, arrives Praslin 2pm.

The "La Belle Edna": Mon., Wed. and Fri.; departs La Digue 6am, arrives Mahé 9.30am; departs Mahé 1pm, arrives La Digue 4.30pm.

The "La Belle Vue": Tues. and Fri.; departs La Digue 6am, arrives Mahé 9.15am; departs Mahé 1pm, arrives La Digue 4.15pm.

The crossing from Praslin to La Digue by the schooners "La Silhouette", "Lady Mary" and "Idéal" takes no more than half an hour. Departure times: Praslin–La Digue: daily, 7.30, 10/10.30, 11.30am, 3.30 and 5.30pm. La Digue–Praslin: daily, 9.30, 10.30am, 2.30 and 5pm.

Information

"La Belle Edma". Tel. 34313

"La Belle Praslinoise". Tel. 33238/335126

William Rose Interisland Service Praslin–La Digue
Baie St Anne/Praslin
Tel. 33229/33859; Telex 2345 COCO SZ

Books

Some bookshops and general stores on Mahé, Praslin and La Digue stock English and French titles.

NPCS (National Printing and Computer Service);
Huteau Lane
Victoria
Tel. 22665/22603/22608
Open: Mon.–Fri. 9am–4.45pm, Sat. 9am–noon;
Pirates Arms Building
Independence Avenue
Victoria
Tel. 24908

Bookshops on
Mahé

Buses

Bus services are operated by the Seychelles Public Transport Corporation (SPTC).

There are bus routes linking Victoria with every settlement and hotel on the island, and even the most distant beaches can be reached by this cheap form of transport. The services from Victoria are:

Mahé

    1 Anse aux Pins
    2 Anse Royal
    3 Anse Boileau–Les Cannelles
    4 Anse Boileau–Montagne Posée
    5 Takamaka
    6 Baie Lazare
    7 Pointe La Rue
    8 Airport
   12 La Misère
   13 Port Glaud–La Misère
   14 Port Glaud–Sans Souci
   21 Bel Ombre
   22 Beau Vallon
   23 Glacis–Beau Vallon
   24 Glacis–Anse Étoile
   25 Anse Étoile
   26 La Gogue
   31 Belvedere
   32 Le Niol
   33 Les Mamelles
   34 Mt Buxton
   35 Sans Souci

Services other than from Victoria:
    9 Anse à la Mouche–La Chalette
   10 Anse Gaulettes–Val d'Endor
   11 Anse Boileau–La Misère
   15 Port Glaud–Sans Souci

The bus station in Victoria is in Palm Street, on the corner of 5th June Avenue opposite Unity House. From Sunday to Thursday services run at regular intervals to all parts of the island between 5.20am and 9.30pm, after which there is a reduced night-time service. On Fridays and Saturdays the regular service extends through to 1.30am. Information: tel. 24550.

Praslin's buses follow a route along the coast road from Anse Kerlan via the airport, Grand Anse, Baie Ste Anne and Anse Volbert to Anse Boudin, with

Praslin

buses from Anse Boudin following the same route in reverse. The whole journey takes about 55 minutes.
Depart Anse Kerlan: 6, 7, 9, 10, 11am, 12 noon, 1.30, 4 and 5 pm.
Depart Anse Boudin: 6, 7.15, 9, 10, 11am, 12noon, 1.30, 4 and 5 pm.

Calendar of Events

See Public Holidays

Camping

Camping is not allowed in the Seychelles. Police permission is also required for sleeping on the beach which means in practice that it too is forbidden.

Car and Bicycle Rental

General

Car rental companies in the Seychelles are restricted in the number of vehicles they can own. In consequence an astonishing multiplicity of firms all compete for business in this lucrative market. The most common types of vehicle are Mini Mokes (very popular with tourists), small and medium-sized Japanese saloons (European cars are extremely rare) and Japanese four-wheel drive models (jeeps). For holidays in July/August, over Christmas/New Year or at Easter it is essential to pre-book in the UK as demand for some types of vehicle may be heavy.

Every hotel has an arrangement with one or more car hire companies (which frequently have their own desks in the hotel foyer). It is a good idea to compare prices more widely however. Cars are usually handed over at the hotel.

Check that the car is mechanically sound in the presence of the representative, also the condition of the tyres and brakes. Take a note of the amount of petrol in the tank (usually almost empty); the level should be the same when the car is returned. And make sure there are seat belts (not all hire cars have them).

Filling stations

Bear in mind if planning a longer excursion that Mahé has only a few filling stations and Praslin only two.
On Mahé: in Beau Vallon, at the junction in front of the police station (tel. 47256); in Victoria, next to the law-courts in Francis Rachel Street, very near the clock tower (tel. 24095); at the airport entrance; in Port Glaud, in the Sheraton Hotel drive; in Anse Royal (tel. 71368).

On Praslin: in Grand Anse (tel. 33240); in Baie Ste Anne.
Open: 6am–11pm (some variations possible).

Prices

The cost of car hire (per day) can vary according to the make of car as well as from firm to firm (and tax at 10% is added to the price). Some operators charge almost the same for Mini Mokes, small saloons and jeeps, others price them differently. Chauffeur-driven cars are also available. Hiring a bicycle (Praslin, La Digue) is much better value than hiring a car.

Car rental on Mahé

Alpha Rent A Car

St Claire Building
P.O. Box 643
Victoria
Tel. 22078/47243; Telex 2341 UNICAR SZ

Riverside
P.O. Box 224
Mont Fleuri
Tel. 24511; Telex 2281 AVIS SZ
Desk at airport
Tel. 73045

Avis

P.O. Box 72
Les Mamelles
Tel. 44280/44296; Telex 2399 BUDGAR SZ
Desk at airport
Tel. 73069

Budget
Rent-a-car

Anse aux Pins
Tel. 76829, after business hours tel. 71496

City Car Hire

St Louis
Tel. 23359

Edens's Car Hire

Victoria House (Room 209)
P.O. Box 559
Victoria
Tel. 23303/47018; Telex 2263 EUCARS SZ
Desk at airport

Europcar

P.O. Box 620
Mare Anglais
Tel. 47333/47508

Exotic Car Hire

Revolution Avenue
P.O. Box 600
Victoria
Tel. 22447/22669; Telex 2310 HERTZ SZ
Desk at airport

Hertz

Le Rocher
Tel. 23420, after business hours tel. 44239

Joe's Car Hire

P.O. Box 375
Le Rocher
Tel. 21888

Kobe Cars

P.O. Box 601
Francis Rachel Street
Victoria
Tel. 24404/47632; Telex 2401 KOKO SZ

Koko Car Hire

P.O. Box 361
Les Mamelles
Tel. 23355; Telex 2371 CAR LAW SZ
Desk at airport

Mahé Car Hire

P.O. Box 169
St Louis
Tel. 23005/22366; Telex 2341 UNICAR SZ

Mein's Car Hire

P.O. Box 640
Anse aux Pins
Tel. 76522; Telex 2283 EUROCAR SZ

MS Car Hire

P.O. Box 461
St Louis
Tel. 22923

Nelsons Car Hire

Car and Bicycle Rental

NTA Car Hire
Kingsgate House
P.O. Box 611
Victoria
Tel. 24900; Telex 2356 NTA SZ
Desk at airport

Petit Car Hire
P.O. Box 83
Le Rocher–Les Mamelles
Tel. 44608; Telex 2202 TXAGY SZ

Ram Car Hire
5th June Avenue
P.O. Box 299
Victoria
Tel. 23443

Silversands
Rent A Car
P.O. Box 279
Bel Ombre
Tel. 47060;
in the Plantation Club: tel. 71588

St Louis Car Hire
42 Kingsgate House
P.O. Box 522
Victoria
Tel. 22086; Telex 2376 JEAN SZ
St Louis
Tel. 22270;
Desk at airport

Sunshine Cars
P.O. Box 127
Le Chantier
Tel. 24671

Tropicar
P.O. Box 641
Mont Fleuri
Tel. 23838, after business hours tel. 41382; Telex 2371 CARLAW SZ
Desk at airport
Tel. 73299

Union Vale Car
Hire
P.O. Box 509
Beau Vallon
Tel. 47052, after business hours tel. 47138; Telex 2324 UVCARS SZ

Victoria Car Hire
P.O. Box 640
Anse aux Pins
Tel. 76314, after business hours tel. 76223/71350
Telex 2283 EUCARS SZ
Desk at airport

Car rental on Praslin

Austral Car
Baie Ste Anne
Tel. 32015/32010

Echo Car Hire
Grand Anse
Tel. 33826

Praslin Holiday
Car Rental
Grand Anse
Tel. 33219/33325

Prestige Car Hire
Grand Anse
Tel. 33226

Solace Car Hire
Grand Anse
Tel. 33445/33525

Anse Kerlan
Tel. 33555

Chauffeur-driven cars are available from Tropicar, Hertz, Mein's and Exotic Car Hire, and from other companies by arrangement.

Bicycle hire
Bicycle hire on Praslin:
Anse Volbert Village
Tel. 32071
or from:
Flying Dutchman Hotel, Grand Anse, tel. 33337
Indian Ocean Fishing Club, Grand Anse, tel. 33324

Côte d'Or Bicycle Hire

Bicycle hire on La Digue:
La Passe
Tel. 34353

Despilly's Rent-a-Bicycle

La Passe
Tel. 34350

Tarosa Proprietary & Rent-a-Bicycle

also from:
La Digue Island Lodge, Anse Réunion, tel. 34232/34233

Chemists

There are very few chemists in the Seychelles. The main pharmacy is at the central hospital in Mont Fleuri, tel. 24400;
Open: Mon.–Fri. 8am–6pm, Sat. and Sun. 8am–noon.

Mahé

Victoria also has three private chemist's shops:
Behrams Pharmacy, Mont Fleuri, tel. 23659;
Open: Mon.–Fri. 8.15am–1pm and 2–5.15pm, Sat. 8am–noon.

George Lailam's, Benezet Street, tel. 21733;
Open: Mon.–Fri. 8.15am–noon and 1–5pm, Sat. 8.15am–1pm.

Philip Fock-Heng, Revolution Avenue, tel. 22751;
Open: Mon.–Fri. 8.30am–5pm, Sat. 8.30am–12.30pm.

Pain-killers and other simple medicines are sometimes sold in general stores. Anything else must be obtained from the local hospital:

Praslin and La Digue

Baie Ste Anne, Praslin, tel. 33333;
Open: Mon.–Fri. 8am–4pm, Sat. 8am–noon.

Logan Hospital, La Digue, tel. 34255.

A doctor's prescription is necessary for medicines obtained at hospital pharmacies.

Church Services

Nearly every town and village in the Seychelles has a Catholic church or chapel. Mass is celebrated at the following times:

Catholic mass

Sat. 5pm, Sun. 7am, 9am and 5pm.

On Mahé

On Praslin	Grand Anse: Sun. 8.30 and 10am. Baie Ste Anne: Sun. 8.30 or 10am (alternately).
On La Digue	Sat. 5pm, Sun. 6.30am.
Anglican services	Anglican services are held on both Mahé and Praslin.
On Mahé	Services are held in St Paul's Cathedral, Victoria (corner of Revolution Avenue and Albert Street): Sun. 6.30 and 8.30am.
On Praslin	Grand Anse: on the 1st and 3rd Sunday in the month at 7am, and on the 2nd and 4th Sunday at 8.30am. Baie Ste Anne: on the 1st, 3rd and (if applicable) 5th Sunday in the month at 8.30am. Consolation (Château de Feuilles): on the 2nd and 4th Sunday in the month at 7am. Anse Kerlan: on the 1st and 3rd Sun. in the month at 10 or 10.30am.

Clothing

Casual clothes are worn for almost every occasion. In some hotel bars and restaurants (e.g. Denis Island Lodge) men are required to wear long trousers after 7.30pm. Jacket and tie are optional.
Topless sunbathing is seen on Seychelles beaches nowadays, but nudism is very much frowned upon.

Currency

General	The unit of currency is the Seychelles rupee (SR) equivalent to 100 cents. There are banknotes in denominations of Rs 10, 25, 50 and 100, as well as Rs 1 and 5 and 1, 5, 10 and 25 cent coins.
Exchange rates (variable)	These can be obtained from banks, tourist bureaux and hotels.
Foreign currency regulations	No limit is put on the amount of Seychelles currency which can be taken in or out of the country. The export of foreign currency is also unrestricted (though large sums should always be declared on entry to avoid any problems when leaving).
Traveller's cheques	Traveller's cheques can be changed in banks and hotels; only a few shops and restaurants accept them however. Rates of exchange for cash are less favourable than for traveller's cheques.
Eurocheques	Almost all banks will cash Eurocheques to a value of £150 on production of a Eurocheque card. Larger hotels will also change them, but usually at a much lower rate. Most hotels and many restaurants will accept payment by Eurocheque. Loss of a Eurocheque card should be reported immediately to the bank which issued it (telephone number in cheque wallet). The card will be cancelled on notification of the loss.
Credit cards	Hotels and car rental firms as well as most restaurants and some shops accept at least one or two of the internationally used credit cards (including American Express, Diners Club, Visa, Barclaycard, Master/Eurocard). Denis Island is an exception – payment there must be in cash or by traveller's cheque.

Local currency

Some major credit card companies have local addresses:

American Express c/o TSS
Victoria House
Francis Rachel Street/State House Avenue
Victoria. Tel. 22414

Diners Club, J. K. Parcou
Victoria House
Francis Rachel Street/State House Avenue
P.O. Box 599
Victoria. Tel. 23303

Visa
Barclays Bank International
P.O. Box 167
Victoria. Tel. 24101

Master Card
P.O. Box 579
Victoria. Tel. 23927

Outside normal banking hours (see Banks) money can be changed only at the airport (where bank counters open for international arrivals and departures) or at reception in the larger hotels. Banks follow the official exchange rate set by the government; the rates offered by hotels are usually less favourable.

Changing money

133

Customs Regulations

Arrival	Articles for personal use may be imported duty free into the Seychelles including, in addition to personal effects: 200 cigarettes or 50 cigars or 250g tobacco; 1 litre spirits with more than 22% alcohol content, 1 litre wine; 0.125 litre perfume, 0.25 litre eau de toilette; other dutiable goods to a value of Rs 400 (adults) or Rs 200 (children under eighteen). The import of weapons (including airguns and harpoon guns), munitions and drugs is strictly forbidden, as is the import of seeds, plants, flowers, fruit, vegetables, meat or meat products and tea. Animals are subject to a period of quarantine (see Travel Documents).
Departure	There are no restrictions on what visitors may take out of the country except that a certificate from an authorised dealer is required in the case of any cocos de mer.
Return to the UK	Duty free allowances on returning to the UK include souvenirs to a value of £32. Adults over 17 years of age are also permitted 1 litre spirits (2 litres if less than 22% alcohol) or 2 litres sparkling wine; 2 litres wine; 200 cigarettes or 100 cigarillos or 50 cigars or 250g tobacco. Those over 15 years of age are also allowed 50g perfume, 100g tea or 40g tea extract, 500g coffee or 200g coffee powder.
Foreign currency	See Currency

Diplomatic Representation

In Great Britain	Seychelles High Commission Eros House (2nd floor) 111 Baker Street London W1M 1FE Tel. (071) 224 1670
In United States	Embassy Suite 927 F 820 Second Avenue, New York Tel. 687 9766
In the Seychelles	British High Commission Victoria House P.O. Box 161 Mahé Tel. 23055/23056; telex 2269 United States of America High Commission Victoria House P.O. Box 251 Mahé Tel. 23921

Diving and Snorkelling

See Sport

Diving Grounds

Sainte Anne Marine National Park	The best diving in and around the principal island, Mahé, is found among the islands of the Sainte Anne Marine National Park (Cerf Island, Long Island, Moyenne, Round Island and Ste Anne). The diving season lasts throughout the year and the waters here are particularly rich, with a great

Sun anemones

variety of fish and coral. Granite outcrops, steep sided reefs, flat coral beds and seaweed all contribute to a wonderfully diverse submarine landscape.

Thanks to the almost continuous bank of coral fringing this part of the coast there is also good diving in Beau Vallon Bay and off the extreme north-west of Mahé – particularly the area between North Point and the Sunset Guest House, including around the little island of L'Îlot. The reefs south of the Sunset Hotel, and those from Fisherman's Cove Hotel westwards to beyond Danzilles, are eminently suitable for inexperienced divers and snorkellers. April to November are the best months for diving here – this being the lee side of the island during the south-east monsoon and the sea in consequence being relatively calm. Other places with good diving are Police Bay in the south, Thérèse Island off the north-west coast, and Petite Anse and Anse Soleil in the south-west.

Mahé

The superb coral reefs protecting Praslin's two longer sides have most to offer divers. There are a number of good spots for snorkelling off Anse Petit Cœur and eastwards of Anse Possession (though a boat is needed to reach them). Especially around the little island of St Pierre, and in the bay at Anse Volbert, the clear shallow waters teem with exquisitely coloured fish. Off Curieuse Island, separated from Praslin by only a narrow channel, the water is again clear and without strong currents, ideal for the less experienced diver.

Praslin

The Ave Maria Rocks, 2km south of La Digue, provide excellent diving, as do the Channel Rocks between La Digue and Round Island (Praslin), the twin islands of Grande and Petite Sœur north-west of La Digue (privately owned, landing fee payable), and the Albatross Rocks north-east of Félicité. All can be reached easily by boat.

La Digue

The waters of Silhouette's north-east coast teem with eye-catching fish, and being particularly clear lend themselves to underwater photography. There are relatively few corals however.

Silhouette

135

The "Ennerdale"	The wreck of the "Ennerdale", which lies near Mamelles, a rocky islet between Mahé and Praslin, is a favourite site for diving. The tanker ran onto the submerged rocks here in 1970. Her cargo of oil had to be blown up by British Navy divers.
Aride	Together with its surrounding waters the granite island of Aride has been declared a nature conservation area and is protected from any form of human interference. Not far from Aride, on the edge of the Mahé Plateau, there is a spectacular outer reef which plunges steeply into the depths.
Frégate	On privately owned Frégate good conditions are found for snorkelling and underwater photography off the beach south of the landing pier. At low tide the waters of Anse Parc are exceptionally still – again excellent for snorkelling. Chimney Rocks on the other hand, off the north of the island, can only be recommended in calm weather and then only for experienced divers. Sharks and big barracuda are often to be seen off Frégate's south-east coast, where the rocks fall sharply away.
Bird and Denis	Close to Bird and Denis, the two coral islands on the Mahé Plateau, the sea floor drops away abruptly to 100m (and to 1800m soon afterwards). The outer reef at Bird is pitted at depths of about 23m with underwater caverns, alive with fish and coral. Similar "caves" are found at depths of only three to seven metres among Denis' deeply fissured coral banks. Smallish sharks, sting-rays and turtles can all be seen here from time to time.
Amirantes	Last but not least good conditions for snorkelling and underwater photography can be enjoyed on the flat coral banks around the Amirantes (Desroches, Poivre, Rémire). There is also excellent diving on the outer reef.

Electricity

The voltage in the Seychelles is 240 volts, 50 cycles AC. Sockets are of the type also used in the UK. Most hotel rooms are fitted with standard European razor sockets. If necessary adaptors can be obtained from hotels or local shops.

Emergencies

Emergency tel. numbers	Dial 999 anywhere in the Seychelles for fire, police, ambulance or doctor.

Excursions and Tour Operators

Excursions	A wide range of excursions is available on and between the islands of the Seychelles. Among the most popular are the bus tours on Mahé, boat trips to various uninhabited islands, visits to the National Parks, island hopping by plane, and exploration of Mahé and Praslin by car. Anyone planning to stay on Mahé and/or Praslin for the duration of their holiday should be sure to take at least one day trip to La Digue, Bird, Cousin or one of the other smaller islands.
Packages	Some tour operators combine several of the excursions listed into a single "package" (e.g. a trip in a glass bottomed boat, a drive around Mahé, and a Seychelles evening, all on the same day).
By bus	Day or half day bus tours are organised by local tour operators, taking in Mahé's main sights (the ruins of the old mission, Anse Boileau, Takamaka,

the tea estate, the botanic gardens, and Victoria). They can be booked at travel agents (or at their desks in the larger hotels). Full day excursions usually include lunch (generally Creole cuisine) with a reduction of up to 50% for children).

The following is a selection of the tours available on Mahé: Mahé tour (full day), north Mahé tour (half day), south Mahé tour (half day), highlands tour (half day, perhaps with a visit to the botanic gardens), tour of Victoria market (combined e.g. with a boat trip to the Sainte Anne Marine National Park or a walk in the hills).

There are excursions to the Sainte Anne Marine National Park – often in modern, semi-submersible and glass bottomed Panorama boats – to the coral grounds of Ste Anne, Cerf, Moyenne, Cachée, Round and Long islands. Lunch is generally taken at a restaurant on one of the islands and time may be set aside for bathing or snorkelling.

By boat and plane

Boat trips are also organised from Mahé to Silhouette, Thérèse, Conception and L'Islette (from Beau Vallon Bay), to North Island (October to April only), Aride (November to May only), and to Praslin and La Digue (sometimes one way by plane). In addition there are mini "sunset" cruises around north Mahé (night-time or evening cruises including transfer, cocktails, barbecue and music).

From Praslin the crossing to La Digue takes just half an hour by ferry or by the schooners "Lady Mary", "La Silhouette" and "Ideal". There are daily excursions from Praslin's west coast to the bird sanctuary on Cousin and from Praslin's east coast to the Curieuse Marine National Park. A visit to Cousin during the sea bird breeding season (April and May) is not to be missed. To minimise disturbance access is restricted to three days a week (Tuesdays, Fridays and Saturdays) with no more than 20 people being allowed at a time. Other excursions from Praslin include visits to Aride (daily from November to May), Félicité, Cocos Island, Marianne and Frégate, with boat trips around Praslin itself a further option.

A supply boat between La Digue and Praslin

Excursions and Tour Operators

Short excursions to St Pierre (several times a day from Anse Volbert), daily bus tours of the island, and visits to the Vallée de Mai National Park are also laid on by the hotels and the three local travel agencies on Praslin. The schooners "Stella Polaris" and "Aurore" are available for group charter. Further information can be obtained from the hotels.

Boat charter

On Mahé, Praslin, La Digue, Denis, Bird, Desroches and Frégate motor boats can be hired for excursions or big game fishing. Yachts and schooners (with from two to ten berths) and catamarans (reasonably priced) can also be chartered for trips lasting several days or weeks (see Sport for the relevant addresses). Many hotels have their own boats for hire.

By plane (island hopping)

Island hopping excursions by plane on the small aircraft belonging to Air Seychelles are becoming increasingly popular. Flights between the main islands are quick and reliable and give holidaymakers who do not want to change hotels the chance of a day trip to other islands in the group.

The possibilities include: bus tour of south Mahé with flight round the island (half day); Praslin (full day); Praslin and La Digue (plane/boat, full day); Praslin and Cousin (plane/boat, full day); Bird Island (with overnight stay at Bird Island Lodge); Frégate (full day).

There are regular charter flights to the coral islands on aircraft belonging to Air Seychelles (payment in some cases being made direct to the organising hotel).

Flights over the islands can also be arranged privately.
Reservations: tel. 73101 or at travel agents (see below).

For holders of a pilot's licence there are flying facilities at the airport-based Aero Club (tel. 76520).

Hiring a car

A hire car is the ideal means of transport for exploring Mahé. Half-open Mini Mokes are much the most popular vehicles for this purpose, but cars of all sizes are available (see Car and Bicycle Rental). Be vigilant though, especially on the beach. Open cars are an invitation to thieves who are unfortunately to be found in the Seychelles just as they are elsewhere. Lack of care can lead to the loss of money, valuables and documents. On Praslin and La Digue hiring a bicycle has many advantages over hiring a car.

Taxi tours

Taxis can be hired by the hour or the day – a useful alternative to self-drive for those nervous about finding their way on the often poorly signposted roads (see Taxis).

Diving trips

See Sport

Travel agents

On Mahé

National Travel Agency (NTA)
Kingsgate House (Pirates Arms Building)
Independence Avenue
P.O. Box 611
Victoria
Tel. 24900; Telex 2356 NTA SZ; Fax. 25111

Mason Travel
Michel Building
Revolution Avenue
P.O. Box 459
Victoria
Tel. 22642; Telex 2230 MASONS SZ; Fax. 21273

Travel Services Seychelles (TSS) Ltd.
Victoria House
State House Avenue
P.O. Box 356
Victoria
Tel. 22414; Telex 2234 LINWES SZ/2247 TRAVSY SZ; Fax. 21366;
Airport office: tel. 73017

Delhomme Air Travel
Kingsgate House (Pirates Arms Building)
Independence Avenue
P.O. Box 611
Victoria
Tel. 22253
(do not organise trips of their own, but will make reservations)

Bunson Travel
Revolution Avenue
P.O. Box 336
Victoria
Tel. 22682/22292; Telex 2216 MASHIP SZ

Reservation Centre Bird & Denis
P.O. Box 404
Victoria
Tel. 24925/25074

For boat trips also:
Marine Charter Association
P.O. Box 469
Victoria
Tel. 22126; Telex 2359 SZ

Mason Travel   On Praslin
Restaurant Britannia
Grand Anse
Tel. 33211; Fax. 33455

NTA
Airstrip–Amitié
Tel. 33223

TSS
Amitié
Tel. 33438; Telex 2385 LINWES SZ; Fax. 33340

La Digue Island Lodge
Anse La Réunion
Tel. 34233

Ferries

See Boat Services

Food and Drink

The local Creole cooking is a mixture of French, Indian, Chinese, African   General
and British influences. The basic ingredients are rice and fish, the main
spices curry and turmeric. Other much favoured spices include cloves,
cinnamon, ginger, chillis, cardamom, mace and nutmeg. Garlic and mint
are often used as well.

Fish

Fish is one of the staple dishes of the islands, beef and chicken being almost as common (pork rather less so). Tuna, sword fish, shark, shellfish, lobster, spiny lobster and crayfish can all be bought on the market in Victoria. The bright red bourgeois or red snapper and various kinds of parrotfish are also very popular. The usual ways of preparing fish are: grilled fish steaks, curried fish ("carry", often very highly spiced), and fish steamed in banana and coconut palm leaves. The favourite among local dishes is "kat-kat de poisson" made from fish, bananas and coconut milk.

Fruit and vegetables

Typical fruit and vegetable dishes almost always feature on the menu. These include "chatinis" (chutneys made from finely chopped or grated fruit or vegetables fried in oil) and "daubes" (fruit stewed in coconut milk). There are 15 or 17 different kinds of bananas and a variety of fresh tropical fruit depending on the season.

Two dishes are considered particular delicacies. One is a dessert, made from the sweet jelly of the not yet ripe coco de mer coconut. The other is "millionaire's salad", made from the green part of the palmiste palm trunk immediately below the leaf shoot. The whole palm is sacrificed to produce this salad – which explains how the dish acquired its name. Felling palms is prohibited nowadays so millionaire's salad can only be enjoyed when a tree has fallen naturally. Each palm yields enough for just ten portions.

Local specialities

Among the more unusual local specialities are "carry de chauve souris" (curried bat), "fricassée d'œufs d'oiseaux" (birds' egg fricassée) and "carry coco d'œufs d'oiseaux" (curried birds' eggs with coconut). Tern's eggs are especially favoured by the Seychellois for the latter dish. Turtle meat or "caille" also features on menus from time to time, the turtle having been cooked in its own shell. Desserts made with coconut, vanilla and bananas (caramelised) are particularly delicious.

Drinks

"Calou" (made from the juice of unripe coconuts) and "bacca" (made from pineapples) are two "native" alcoholic drinks enjoyed by the Seychellois. But here as elsewhere beer has become more and more popular in recent years.

Restaurants

See entry

Galleries

See Museums and Galleries

Getting to the Seychelles

By plane

Air Seychelles has 5 flights a week from London to Mahé via Paris, Frankfurt or Rome. British Airways also fly from London, either direct or with a stopover, and there are Air France flights from Paris (en route to Mauritius and/or Réunion).

Alitalia, Aeroflot and half a dozen African and Asian airlines also run services to the Seychelles (Alitalia only in the season).
There are flight connections to and/or from Jiddah, Abu Dhabi, Nairobi, Mauritius, Réunion, Moscow, Larnaca, Aden, Dar es Salaam, Singapore, Bahrain, Athens, Maseru, Dhahran and Dubai.

Seychelles government policy is to discourage mass tourism and keep a tight check on numbers. Charter flights from Europe are on a very limited basis therefore and confined to the very busiest times.

Information can be obtained from Air Seychelles office in UK.

Europa office:
Suite 6, Kelvin House
Kelvin Way
Crawley, West Sussex RH10 2SE
Tel. (0044/293) 536313; Fax. (0044/293) 562353

The sea passage to Mahé by freighter from Mombasa (Kenya) or Bombay   By ship
(India) takes a few days. Further information can be obtained from the
shipping companies in Victoria (Mahé):

Hunt, Deltel & Co.
P.O. Box 14
Tel. (00248) 22109; Telex (956) 2249 SZ; Fax. (00248) 23867

Mahé Shipping Co.
P.O. Box 336
Tel. (00248) 22708; Telex (965) 216 MASHIP SZ; Fax. (00248) 22978

Golf

See Sport

Health and Health Regulations

Travellers arriving in the Seychelles from Europe do not need vaccination
certificates. Those coming from infected areas (which include a number of
African and Asian countries) must however show proof of vaccination
against yellow fever and cholera. For further information contact:

Principal Immigration Officer
P.O. Box 430
Victoria. Tel. 73325/22881

It is important not to underestimate the risk of sunburn. Sun-cream (with a   Sunburn
high protective factor), sun-glasses and a sun-hat are an essential part of
every tourist's luggage. Particular care should be taken when snorkelling.
The sun's rays are even more dangerous when reflected off the water so
wear a T-shirt at all times. Sea urchins, found on many beaches, are
another problem; bathing shoes should be worn to avoid painful stings.
Wounds caused by coral must be carefully disinfected – many species
excrete a form of poison. And keep a particular look-out for stonefish when
wading in the shallow waters of the lagoons. They blend in perfectly with
the greyish-brown background and their sting can prove fatal (so too can
contact with a firefish). In either case seek medical attention immediately.

Help for the Disabled

Wheelchairs are available at the airport for arriving and departing visitors.
For the duration of their stay they can borrow a wheelchair from the central
hospital at Mont Fleuri, Victoria, tel. 24400.

The hotels most suitable for disabled people are: Hotels
The Reef Hotel, Beau Vallon Bay Hotel, Coral Strand Hotel and the Plantation Club (all on Mahé). Some of their bedrooms are on the ground floor.

Disabled people should always make their requirements fully known when   **N.B.**
booking a room.

Hotels

General	There are a total of 3616 tourist beds available in the Seychelles (with another 880 in the pipeline or planned). Of these, 2800 are on Mahé, 535 on Praslin and 88 on La Digue. Bird and Denis have about 50 beds each and the remaining 100 or so are spread between the other islands. Guest houses are generally private homes adapted to accommodate guests, and often furnished in a highly individualistic manner. Like hotels many guest houses have restaurants, and on Mahé in particular non-residents are usually welcome for meals.
Prices	Hotel prices range from Rs 345/460 for a single and Rs 890/970 for a double room with breakfast in the low season, to Rs 660/830 and Rs 1720 during the peak holiday periods. (Low season is from May to July, peak periods are at Christmas and Easter, mid season covers the rest of the year.)
Central booking	There is a central booking service for hotels and apartments belonging to the Seychelles Hotels group: Seychelles Hotels P.O. Box 550 Victoria Tel. 47141; Telex 2272 SHL SZ; Fax. 47606 On Praslin the Equator and Paradise hotels and the Auberge Club also belong to a booking chain. Reservations are interchangeable between the three providing suitable rooms are available.
N.B.	In the list which follows numbers in brackets are for bedrooms in the larger hotels (no number is given for hotels with fewer than 20). Abbreviations: G=guest house, A=apartments
Amirantes group	See Desroches
On Bird	Bird Island Lodge (25), G, P.O. Box 404, tel. 24925/44449, telex 2334 BIRD SZ
On Denis	Denis Island Lodge (25), tel. 44143, fax. 44405 (reservations: P.O. Box 404, tel. 23392, telex 2319 DENIS SZ)
On Desroches	Desroches Island Lodge (20), tel. (00873) 1664101
On Frégate	Plantation House, G, P.O. Box 330, tel. 23123/24789, telex 2406 ROBIN SZ, fax. 25169
On La Digue	*La Digue Island Lodge (35), Anse La Réunion, tel. 34232/34233, telex 2292 GREGLIO SZ Bernique's Guest House, G, tel. 34229 Choppy's Bungalows, G, Anse La Réunion, tel. 34334 Jouc d'Or Guest House, G, tel. 34250/34247
On Mahé	North-west coast: *Le Méridien–Fisherman's Cove Hotel (48), P.O. Box 35, Bel Ombre, tel. 47252, telex 2296 SZ, fax. 47540 Auberge Club des Seychelles (41), P.O. Box 526, Danzilles, tel. 47550, telex 2323 CAUSEY SZ, fax. 47703 Beau Vallon Bungalows, Relais des Îles, Beau Vallon, tel. 47382 Beau Vallon Hotel (Seychelles Hotels; 184), P.O. Box 550, Beau Vallon, tel. 47141, telex 2372 BEAU SZ, fax. 47107 Coral Strand Hotel (103), P.O. Box 400, Beau Vallon, tel. 47036, telex 2215 CORAL SZ, fax. 47517 Coco d'Or Guest House, G, Beau Vallon, tel. 47331, telex 2325 CODOR SZ Le Tamarinier, Relais des Îles, G, Bel Ombre, tel. 47611, fax. 47711

Coral Strand Hotel and its swimming-pool (Mahé)

Panorama Guest House, G, Beau Vallon–Mare Anglaise, P.O. Box 167, tel. 47300, telex 2266 PANRAM SZ
Villa Madonna, G, Beau Vallon, tel. 47403
Villa Napoleon, G, P.O. Box 5, Beau Vallon, tel. 47133
Bel Ombre Holiday Villas, P.O. Box 528, Bel Ombre, tel. 47616
Vacoa Village (Seychelles Hotels), A, Beau Vallon–Mare Anglais, tel. 47130

North and north-east coast:
*Sunset Beach Hotel (25), P.O. Box 372, Glacis, tel. 47227, telex 2344 SUNSET SZ, fax. 47521
Northholme Hotel (Seychelles Hotels; 19, and more planned), P.O. Box 333, Glacis, tel. 47225, telex 2355 COSNOR SZ, fax. 47219
Vista Bay Club (33), P.O. Box 622, Glacis, tel. 47351, telex 2318 VISMAR SZ, fax. 47261
Villa Carol, P.O. Box 522, Glacis, tel. 41445
Clos des Roses, G, Anse Étoile, tel. 41245
Manresa, G, Anse Étoile, tel. 41388, telex 2389 SZ
North Point Guest House, G, Fond des Lianes, Machabée, tel. 41339
Les Manguiers, A, Machabée, tel. 41455/47167

Victoria and central Mahé:
Abbéville Guest House, G, La Misère, P.O. Box 167
Auberge Louis XVII, G, La Louise, La Misère Road, P.O. Box 807, tel. 44411, fax. 44428
Beaufond Lane Guest House, G, P.O. Box 140, Mont Fleuri, tel. 22408 and 24566
Belle Vue, G, Pointe Conan, P.O. Box 543
Eureka Guest House, G, La Louise, P.O. Box 193, tel. 44349
Harbour View Guest House, G, Mont Fleuri, P.O. Box 631, tel. 22473
Hill Top, G, Serret Road, St Louis, tel. 23553
Le Niol Guest House, G, Le Niol, P.O. Box 591, tel. 23262

Le Surcouf Hotel, G, Pointe Conan, P.O. Box 657, tel. 41175

Marie-Antoinette, G, Serret Road, tel. 23942

Pension Bel Air, G, Bel Air, P.O. Box 116, tel. 24416, fax. 24923

Seabreeze Guest House, G, Pointe Conan, tel. 41021

Sunrise Guest House, G, Mont Fleuri, P.O. Box 615, tel. 24836/24560, telex 2201 SZ

Timbertin Lodge, G, Bel Air, P.O. Box 94, Curio Road, telex 2274 SZ

Michel Holiday Apartments, A, P.O. Box 277, Les Mamelles, tel. 44540, telex 2230 MASON SZ

East coast:

* Reef Hotel (Seychelles Hotels; 150), P.O. Box 388, Anse aux Pins, tel.76691, telex 2231 REEF SZ, fax. 76296

Bougainville Guest House, G, P.O. Box 378, Anse Royal, tel. 71334, telex 2327 BOUVIL SZ

Carefree Guest House, G, Anse aux Pins, P.O. Box 403, tel. 76237

Casuarina Beach Hotel, G, Anse aux Pins, P.O. Box 338, tel. 76211, telex 2321 CARINA SZ

Lalla Panzi, G, Anse aux Pins, tel. 76411

La Retraite, G, Anse aux Pins, tel. 76816

La Roussette, G, Anse aux Pins, tel. 76245

Rose Cottage, G, Pointe au Sel, tel. 71434

Villa Maria, G, Cascade, tel. 73046

West and south-west coast:

* Equator Grand Anse Residence Hotel (60), P.O. Box 526, Grand Anse–La Béolière, tel. 78228, telex 2277 EQUSEY SZ, fax. 78244

* Le Méridien–Barbarons Beach Hotel (125), P.O. Box 626, Barbarons, tel. 78253, telex 2258, BBCH SZ, fax. 78484

* Seychelles Sheraton Hotel (formerly Mahé Beach Hotel; 173), P.O. Box 540, Port Glaud, tel. 78451, telex 2245 SHER SZ, fax. 78517

* The Plantation Club (formerly Intercontinental Seychelles; 206), P.O. Box 437, Val Mer, tel. 71588, telex 2383 PCLUB SZ, fax. 71517

* Blue Lagoon Chalets, A, Anse à la Mouche, tel. 71197, fax. 71565

Auberge d'Anse Boileau, Anse Boileau, P.O. Box 211, tel. 76660, telex 2248 EMOBOI SZ

Château d'Eau, G, Domaine de Barbarons, P.O. Box 107, tel. 78577, telex 2398 CHADAU SZ

Lazare Picault, G, Baie Lazare, P.O. Box 135, tel. 71117, telex 2298 PICO SZ

L'Islette, G, Port Glaud–L'Islette Island, P.O. Box 349, tel. 78229

On Moyenne   Maison Moyenne, G, P.O. Box 577, Moyenne Island

On Praslin   * Château de Feuilles, Pointe Cabris, tel. 33316, telex 2255 CABRIS SZ

* L'Archipel, Anse Gouvernement, tel. 32242, telex 2345 COCO SZ, fax. 32072

Côte d'Or Lodge (Club Vancanze; 28), P.O. Box 388, Côte d'Or, tel. 32200, telex 2246 COTDOR SZ, fax. 32130

Flying Dutchman (Seychelles Hotels), Grand Anse, tel. 33337, telex 2336 SZ

La Réserve, Anse Petite Cour, tel. 32211, telex 2360 RESERV SZ, fax. 32166

Maison des Palmes, Amitié, tel. 33411, telex 2326 PALMES SZ, fax 33880

Paradise Hotel (42), Anse Volbert, tel. 32255, telex 2251 PARADI SZ, fax. 32019

Praslin Beach Hotel (Seychelles Hotels; 77), Côte d'Or, Anse Volbert, tel. 32144, telex 2250 PBH SZ, fax 32244

Chauve Souris Island Lodge, G, Chauve Souris Island, Côte d'Or, tel. 32003, telex 2345 SZ

Coco Bello, G, Grand Anse, tel. 33320

Colibri Guest House, in the hills

Grand Anse Beach Villa, G, Grand Anse, tel. 33445

Indian Ocean Fishing Club (Seychelles Hotels), G, Grand Anse, P.O. Box 453, tel. 33324/33457, telex 2201 TXAGI SZ

Merry Crab, G, Grand Anse
Orange Tree House, G, Baie Ste Anne, tel. 33248
The Britannia, G, Grand Anse, tel. 33215, fax 33944
The Fish Trap, G, Baie Ste Anne
Village du Pêcheur, G, Côte d'Or, tel. 32030, telex 2394 VILLAGE SZ,
fax 32185

Silhouette Island Lodge, tel. 24003, telex 2396 SILLOD SZ, fax 41178 **On Silhouette**

Information

Seychelles Tourist Office
Eros House (2nd floor)
111 Baker Street
London W1M 1FE
Tel. (071) 224 1670 **In Great Britain**

Seychelles Tourist Office
Independence House
Independence Avenue
P.O. Box 92, Victoria (Mahé)
Tel. 25333; Telex 2275 SEYTOB SZ; Fax. 24035 **In the Seychelles**

UNIQUE BY A THOUSAND MILES

The Tourist Office's responsibilities extend over every island, village and
settlement in the Seychelles.
Open: Mon.–Fri. 8am–noon and 1.30–4pm.

Information desks at Mahé International Airport, tel. 73136, and Praslin
airport, tel. 33346.

For information about islands not developed for tourism:
Island Development Company Ltd.
P.O. Box 638
Victoria (Mahé). Tel. 21369/21370

Insurance

Visitors are strongly advised to ensure that they have adequate holiday
insurance, including loss or damage to luggage, loss of currency and
jewellery. General

It is essential for visitors to take out some form of short-term health
insurance providing complete cover and possibly avoiding delays. Health

Visitors intending to hire a car should ensure that their insurance is comprehensive and covers driving in the Seychelles. Vehicles

See also Travel Documents.

Language

Some useful Creole words and phrases (the pronunciation resembles
French):

Good morning, good day, hello	Bonzour
Good evening	Bonswar
Good-bye	Orevwar
Yes	Wi

No	Non
Please	Silvouple
Thank you, thank you very much	Mersi, mersi bokou
How are you?	Koman sava? Ki i dir?
I am well, thank you. And you?	Mon byen, mersi. Oumenm?
What is your name?	Koman ou apele?
My name is . . .	Mon apel . . .
I don't understand	Mon pa konpran
Where is the bank, please?	Oli labank silvouple?
. . . the market	. . . bazar
. . . the bar	. . . bar
. . . the key	. . . mon lakle
. . . my room	. . . mon lasanm
. . . my luggage	. . . mon bagaz
Bon appetit	Bon apetit
That is nice	Sa i zoli
A coffee, please	En kafe, silvouple
A beer, . . .	En labyer, . . .
The menu, . . .	Meni, . . .
The bill, . . .	Bil, . . .
Where do you live?	Kote ou reste?
How much is that?	Konbyen sa?
	Konbyen mon dwa ou?
Excuse me, do you have a light, please?	Eskiz mwan, ou annan dife, silvouple?
What is the time, please?	Keler i ete, silvouple?
When does the plane leave, please?	Keler avyon i kite, silvoulpe?
When does the boat leave?	Keler bato i ale?
Is that our boat?	Nou bato sa?
. . . bus	. . . bis
What is this beach called?	Komanyer sa lans i apele?
What is this fish called?	Komanyer sa pwason i apele?
May I use the phone, please?	Mon kapa servi telefonn, silvouple?
When does the bar close?	Keler bar i fermen?
Would you like to dance?	Oule danse?
Can I change money here?	Mon kapa sanz larzan isi, silvouple?
The key, please	Lakle lasanm, silvouple
Where can I buy stamps?	Kote mon kapa aste tenm?
Nil	zero
One	en
Two	de
Three	trwa
Four	kat
Five	senk
Six	sis
Seven	set
Eight	uit
Nine	nef
Ten	dis
Tomorrow	demen
The day after tomorrow	apredemen
Yesterday	yer
In the morning(s)	bomaten
In the evening(s)	aswar
Monday	lendi
Tuesday	mardi
Wednesday	mekredi
Thursday	zedi
Friday	wandredi
Saturday	samdi
Sunday	dimans

Libraries

Library facilities in the Seychelles:
National Library (Libreri Nasyonal)
State House Avenue
Victoria
Tel. 21072
Open: 8.30am–5pm, Sat. 8.30–11.45pm.
The library contains mainly biographies and a selection of English and French literature. A new building is planned.
There is a branch on Praslin (at the school in Baie Ste Anne) tel. 33524
La Digue's public library is in the school at La Réunion.

Many hotels have a selection of novels in English, French and (sometimes) other languages, mostly left behind by previous guests.   Note

Maps

Hildebrand's holiday map "Seychelles" (general map with details of various islands).   1:6,000,000

All sorts of maps can bought from the shop called: **N.B.**
Brigade Hydrographique et Topographique des Seychelles
Independence House
Independence Avenue
Victoria
Tel. 32606

Medical Assistance

The Seychelles (Mahé, Praslin, La Digue) have an efficient health service employing 37 doctors, 31 dentists, psychiatrists and other skilled medical staff. There are 373 hospital beds available for use by the islanders and visitors. All the doctors speak English and/or French. On Mahé the central hospital at Victoria operates an ambulance service. Patients from other islands in need of urgent medical attention are taken to hospital in Victoria by air. The emergency telephone number (999) is the same for all the islands.   General

The central hospital (with dental clinic) is situated in Victoria's Mont Fleuri suburb, on the main road to the airport, tel. 24400.   Mahé

In addition every village/district on Mahé has its own smaller clinic:
Anse Royal, tel. 71222
Anse aux Pins, tel. 76535
Anse Boileau, tel. 76649
Baie Lazare Village, tel. 71151
Beau Vallon, tel. 24400 (via the central hospital)
Béolière, tel. 78259
Corgat Estate, tel. 24400 (via the central hospital)
English River, tel. 24400 (via the central hospital)
Glacis, tel. 24400 (via the central hospital)
Les Mamelles, tel. 24400 (via the central hospital)
Port Glaud, tel. 78223
Takamaka, tel. 71231

Medical Assistance

Praslin	The hospital on Praslin is at Baie Ste Anne, at the junction of the road to the Vallée de Mai National Park, tel. 33333.
	There are two smaller clinics on Praslin as well, at Grand Anse (tel. 33414) and Anse Kerlan.
La Digue	La Digue also has its own hospital, the Logan Hospital, tel. 34255.
Hotel medical service	Special medical arrangements exist for foreign visitors staying in the islands' hotels. These include:
Mahé	On Mahé: a doctor's visit and/or treatment at the central hospital either by appointment or during regular consulting hours (Mon.–Fri. 8am–noon), tel. 24400. Alternatively (if more convenient) treatment at the nearest clinic (see list above), consulting hours Mon.–Fri. 8am–4pm, Sat. 8am–noon. Requests for a doctor to call at the hotel (visiting hours: Mon.–Fri. 2–6pm) should be made through reception or direct to the central hospital, tel. 24400. In an emergency visits will also be made after 6pm and at weekends.
Praslin and La Digue	On Praslin and La Digue: consultations by appointment at the nearest clinic (see list above), Mon.–Fri. 8am–4pm, Sat. 8pm–noon. Both islands have an emergency medical service which comes into operation on weekdays after 4pm and after midday Sat. (for the whole weekend), tel. 33333 (Praslin) or 34255 (La Digue).
	Consultations have to be paid for in cash. When a doctor visits an hotel, on the other hand, payment is made to the hotel. A receipt is issued for all payments.
	See also Insurance

Museum and Galleries (Mahé)

Museums in Victoria	National Archives La Bastille (north of Victoria) Tel. 21931 Open: Mon.–Fri. 8am–4pm, Sat. 8am–noon
	National Museum Independence Avenue Victoria Tel. 23653 Open: Mon.–Fri. 7am–5pm, Sat. 9am–noon
	Political Museum (SPPF) Francis Rachel Street Victoria Tel. 24251
	Christy's Art Gallery Quinssy Street Victoria Tel. 21019 Open: Mon.–Fri. 9am–5pm, Sat. 9am–3pm
	Galerie d'Art No 1 Mahé Trade Building State House Avenue Victoria Tel. 22856

Michael Adams
P.O. Box 405, Mahé
Anse aux Poules Bleues
Tel. 71106
Open: Mon.–Fri. 9am–4pm, Sat. 9am–noon
(or by prior telephone arrangement)

Tom Bowers (sculptures)
Les Cannelles Road
Sancta Maria Estate. Tel. 71518

Gérard Devoud Studio
Les Mamelles. Tel. 47280
Open: 8am–8pm

Galleries outside
Victoria

Newspapers and Periodicals

English and French news magazines (Time, Newsweek, L'Express, Le Point, Le Nouvel Observateur) and weekly editions of the "Guardian" and "Le Monde" are available in hotels and bookshops.

The best selection of foreign newspapers is found in shops belonging to the National Printing and Computer Service (NPCS):
National Printing and Computer Service
Huteau Lane and Independence Avenue (Pirates Arms Building)
Victoria/Mahé
Open: Mon.–Fri. 9am–4.45pm, Sat. 9am–noon

"The Nation", the Seychelles' one daily paper (circulation about 3200) has articles in English, French and Creole. The monthly "Seychelles Today" publishes tourist information in English and French.

Other local publications include the two-monthly periodical "Echo des Îles" and the SPPF's official (monthly) "The People".

Night-life

Seychelles night-life, and the evening entertainment put on by hotels, is very much what might be expected of a quiet holiday destination where the emphasis is on enjoyment of the natural world.

Only the larger hotels at Beau Vallon Bay and on Mahé's west coast have regular evening entertainment – dancing, fashion shows, barbecues and folk evenings ("sega" dancing and Camtole music).

The islands' two casinos are both on Mahé, one in the Plantation Club, the other in the Beau Vallon Bay Hotel. Local people are excluded.

Casinos

There are discothèques on Mahé and Praslin and, in a small way, on La Digue.

Discothèques

On Mahé:
Barrel Disco, Victoria, open Thursday to Saturday
Kaitiolo, Anse aux Pins, tel. 76453
La Perle Noire, Beau Vallon, tel. 47046

Other venues are the Sheraton Hotel (nightly), Coral Strand Hotel (three times a week), Beau Vallon Bay Hotel and Barbarons Hotel (weekends).

On Praslin:
The Lost Horizon (open air), Baie Ste Anne, open Friday to Sunday
Ma belle Amie, Côte d'Or, open Friday and Saturday

In addition dance evenings are arranged by the Paradise and Flying Dutchman hotels and also by the "Coco Bello" restaurant (Saturdays).

On La Digue:
Discothèque in Choppy's Bungalows (at weekends)

Opening Times

Shops	Shops generally open at the following times: Mon.–Fri. 8am–5pm (though some close for lunch between noon and 1 or 1.30pm). Most shops, but not all, open Sat. 8am–noon, and some open on Sunday mornings as well.
Offices	Open: Mon.–Fri. 8am–noon and 1.30–4pm
Chemist's shops	See Chemists
Banks	See entry
Post offices	See Post, Telegraph and Telephone
Filling stations	See Car and Bicycle Rental

Paragliding

See Sport

Police

Emergency calls   The police emergency telephone number (999) is the same on all the islands.
Police headquarters are in Victoria (Revolution Avenue, tel. 22011).
Other police stations on Mahé:

Airport, tel. 73001
Anse aux Pins, tel. 76217
Anse Boileau, tel. 76721
Anse Étoile, tel. 22011 (via police headquarters)
Anse Royal, tel. 71226
Baie Lazare Village, tel. 71130
Beau Vallon, tel. 47242
Cascade, tel. 73316
Glacis, tel. 47241
Mont Fleuri, tel. 22011 (via police headquarters)
New Port, tel. 22011 (via police headquarters)
Port Glaud, tel. 78355
Takamaka, tel. 71249

Police stations on Praslin:
Baie Ste Anne, tel. 33232
Grand Anse, tel. 33251

Police stations on La Digue:
La Passe, tel. 34251

Post and Telephone

Main post office in Victoria (Mahé):
Liberty House, corner of Albert and Independence Street
Tel. 22357
Open: Mon.–Fri. 8am–4pm, Sat. 8am–noon.
Postcards and letters for posting can be left at hotel reception desks.

Main post office

Post for Europe leaves the island once or twice a week; it is normally carried by Air France and routed via Paris. Letters and postcards usually take a week or more to reach their European destination.

Letters and postcards for Europe

Airmail must be handed in at the main post office by noon if it is to leave the country on a flight the same evening or the next morning.

First Class:
An airmail letter to Europe (up to 10g) costs Rs 3, with a further Rs 2 for every additional 10g. Postcards cost Rs 2.

Postal rates

Second Class:
The second class letter rate (up to 20g, by air or surface mail) is Rs 2.

The islands' telephone network meets the highest modern standards with regard to both internal and international calls. Telephone calls to Europe can be made from all the hotels, or by direct dialling from the offices of Cable & Wireless (Francis Rachel Street, in Victoria), or using a phonecard from the public phonecard telephones being installed throughout Mahé. Calls to the UK cost about Rs 30 per minute. Hotels add a surcharge of up to 35%.

Telephone

The code for calls to the UK from the Seychelles is 044, to the United States and Canada 01. The international code should be dialled first followed by the local code (omitting the first 0) and then the subscriber number.

International dialling code

The international dialling code for calls to the Seychelles from the UK is 010 248, from the United States and Canada 011 248. This should be followed by the subscriber number, a local code being needed only in the case of Desroches (00873).

The international telex code is 965.

Cable and Wireless, Francis Rachel Street, Victoria, operate public fax and telex services.

Fax and telex services

Protected Areas and Tours

Aldabra Atoll and the islands of Cousin and Aride are nature reserves and very strictly controlled.

Nature conservation

The Morne Seychellois National Park on Mahé and the Vallée de Mai National Park on Praslin are biosphere reserves, i.e. no economic development is allowed.

The Vallée de Mai on Praslin and the Veuve Réserve on La Digue are officially designated special reserves.

There are also a number of marine National Parks. These include the waters around the Ste Anne group of islands (Ste Anne, Cerf, Moyenne, Round, Long) and those around Baie Ternay/Port Launay (Port Launay National Park) off Mahé, around Curieuse Island off Praslin, and around Silhouette.

Also protected are the Île Cocos near Praslin and the African Banks in the Amirantes.

While the knowledge and experience of a guide can add considerably to the interest and enjoyment, it is not necessary to join a guided tour in order to visit the National Parks. At the Vallée de Mai in particular there are helpful brochures available at the pay-desk.

Guided tours

Public Holidays

January 1st/2nd: New Year
May 1st: Labour Day
June 5th: Liberation Day, with a parade
June 29th: Independence Day, National Youth Sports Festival
August 15th: Assumption, celebrated with much festivity on La Digue
November 1st: All Saints' Day
December 8th: Immaculate Conception
December 25th: Christmas
Good Friday, Easter Saturday, Easter Sunday, Corpus Christi
(As in the UK, if a holiday falls on a Sunday the Monday immediately following is a holiday also.)

Radio and Television

Radio Seychelles broadcasts news in English at 0700, 1200 and 1900 and in French at 0730, 1300 and 2100 (on 219 megahertz medium wave, and 1368 kilohertz).
Radio F.E.B.A (Far East Broadcasting Association) transmits religious pro- grammes to Middle and Far Eastern countries throughout the day (on short wave).

Radio

Radio Television Seychelles is on the air only at weekends (Friday to Sunday from 1700 or 1800 to 2230). There is a news bulletin in English at 1800 and in French at 2030.

Television

Restaurants

In addition to the restaurants listed below, most hotels and many guest houses welcome non-residents for meals.

N.B.

Beach Shed, Cerf Island, tel. 22126, closed Wed., Thur. and Sat.

On Cerf Island

La Digue Island Lodge, Anse Réunion, tel. 34237/34239
Choppy's, Anse Réunion, tel. 34224

On La Digue

North-west:
*La Scala (fish, French-Italian), Bel Ombre, tel. 47535, closed Sun. and in Sept.
*Le Corsaire (French), Bel Ombre, tel. 47171 (Méridien), closed Mon.
Baobab Pizzeria, Beau Vallon, tel. 47167
Beau Vallon Beach Pub, Beau Vallon, tel. 47442
La Perle Noire (Creole and French), Beau Vallon, tel. 47046, closed Wed.
Le Tamarinier (guest house), Bel Ombre, tel. 47611

On Mahé

◀ *In the Vallée de Mai on Praslin*

Restaurants

North-east:
Kyoto Restaurant (Japanese), Anse Étoile, tel. 41337, closed Sun.
Le Kakatwa, Anse Étoile, tel. 41327
Lobster Pot (fish), Pointe Conan, tel. 41376, closed Sun.
Sonah Mahal Indian Restaurant, Anse Étoile, tel. 4117

Victoria and central Mahé:
*Maria Antoinette (Creole), St Louis, tel. 23942, closed Sun.
King Wah Restaurant (Chinese), Benezet Street, Victoria, tel. 23658, closed
Sun.
La Cocoteraie (Seychelles Hotels), Pirates Arms Building, Independence
Avenue, Victoria, tel. 22201, closed Sun.
L'Amiral, Independence House, Victoria, tel. 21500, closed Sun.
La Marmite, Revolution Avenue, Victoria, tel. 22932, closed Sun. lunchtime
and Mon. evenings.
La Moutia (Creole), La Louise, tel. 44433
Le Sapin, Botanic Garden, Victoria, tel. 24760, lunchtime only, closed Sun.
Mandarin Restaurant, Victoria, tel. 22818, lunchtime only, closed Sun.
Pirates Arms Café, Independence Avenue, tel. 25001

South-east:
Katiolo Restaurant, Anse Faure, tel. 76453
Pomme Cannelle (Seychelles Hotels), Anse aux Pins
Ty Foo, Le Cap/Pointe au Sel, tel. 71485

West and south-west:
*Au Capitain Rouge (Provençal), Anse à la Mouche, tel. 71224
*Chez Plum (formerly Chez Philos), Anse Boileau, tel. 76660, closed Mon.
*Islander (formerly Juliana's), Anse à la Mouche, tel. 71289, closed Sun.
and in June.
Chez Baptista's, Takamaka, tel. 71535, lunchtime only
Hoi Tin, Anse Gaulettes, tel. 71159
La Sirène (fish), Anse aux Poules Bleues, tel. 71339, lunchtime only
L'Islette, Port Glaud, tel. 78229
Sundown Restaurant, Port Glaud, tel. 78352, closed Sun.

On Moyenne   Maison Moyenne, tel. 22414, lunchtime only

On Praslin   *Château de Feuilles (French cuisine, hotel restaurant, reservations only),
Pointe Cabris, tel. 33316
Coco Bello (Creole), Grand Anse, tel. 33220
Laurier Restaurant, Anse Volbert, tel. 32241, closed Sun.
Restaurant Britannia (Creole), Grand Anse, tel. 33215
Les Rochers, tel. 33230, closed Sun.

On Round Island   Chez Gaby, Round Island, tel. 22929, closed Mon. and Fri.

Sailing and Boat Hire

See Sport

Souvenirs

Lacking their own tradition in arts and crafts and with items of international
fashion rarely seen on sale, shopping in the Seychelles can hardly be called
exciting. The swim suits and beach robes sold in souvenir shops and hotels
are inexpensive and good value for money, but often of poor quality.

Souvenirs   Most favoured by souvenir hunters are the typically Seychelles "bou-
bous" (lengths of brightly coloured cotton), shells and shellfish, wicker-
work and baskets, cocos de mer (either in their natural state, or polished

Souvenir stall at the Clock Tower, Victoria

smooth and hollowed out to weigh less than 1kg), hats woven from palm or banana leaves and tablemats. Coral and mother-of-pearl jewellery is widely available as well – but remember that every purchase resisted is a positive contribution to nature conservation! – as are ceramics, batiks, woodwork and finally handwork made from shells, coconuts and palm straw. Also very popular as mementoes are the (somewhat macabre) walking sticks made from the back-bones of sharks and the very attractive series of Seychelles stamps.

Avoid buying tortoiseshell bracelets, salad servers or similar articles! These are made from the shell of the hawksbill turtle, or related species, now protected under the Washington agreement designed to safeguard animals threatened with extinction (to which the UK is a signatory). All items of tortoiseshell will be confiscated by British customs on arrival in the UK. Once again, to resist buying is to help protect these rare species of turtle.

Victoria's shopping streets – Independence Avenue, Francis Rachel Street and Albert Street – are all located around the clock tower. In addition there are now souvenir shops virtually everywhere on the three largest islands, Mahé, Praslin and La Digue.

Art and craftwork can be found at:
Seychelles Handicraft Association (Duty Free Building)
Francis Rachel Street
Victoria

Craft shops
(Mahé)

Seychelles Potter's Cooperative (Seypot)
P.O. Box 669
Les Mamelles
Tel. 44080

Postage stamps make popular souvenirs

Ron Gerlach Batiks
P.O. Box 207/Mahé
Shop in Beau Vallon
Open: 10am–5pm

W. Pit Hugelmann (perfume)
P.O. Box 258/Mahé
North East Point
Tel. 41329

Michael Adams (paintings, etchings)
P.O. Box 405/Mahé
Anse aux Poules Bleues
Tel. 71106

Craft Village/Vilaz Artizanal
(large selection of handicrafts)
Anse aux Pins
Closed Mon.

La Marine (handmade model ships)
Le Cap
Tel. 76177

Gérard Devoud (paintings)
P.O. Box 72
Les Mamelles (Budget Car Hire)
Tel. 47280; Telex 2399 SZ

Seychelles Design
Anse aux Pins
Tel. 76134

Sunstroke (textile design)
Tel. 24767

Sport

Together with enjoyment of the natural world sport ranks highly among the attractive leisure options available in the Seychelles. There are facilities in particular for many different types of watersports, for tennis and for golf.

The relatively calm waters of the Seychelles Plateau provide conditions ideal for sea angling. Big game fishing, though a comparative newcomer to the scene, is rapidly gaining in popularity, particularly in the outlying islands. There are some excellent fishing grounds on the Seychelles Plateau, the waters of which abound with fish. Most commonly caught are sail fish, wahoo (*acanthocybium solandri*), several varieties of tuna and bonito (small tuna), barracuda, blue and black marlin and shark. World records have also been set in Seychelles waters for a number of other species (with catches of up to 455kg). The fishing around Denis and Bird islands is especially good because here the edge of the Seychelles bank drops steeply to depths of 1800m. The waters of the lagoons can be fished with a ground line.

Angling and big game fishing

The best months for sea angling and big game fishing are from November through to May; July and August are least favourable, when very rough seas are caused by the south-east monsoon.

Fishing tackle can be bought at:
Anse Royal Marine
P.O. Box 469
Mont Fleuri
Tel. 22851

Catamarans

Hook-N-Nook
Francis Rachel Street
P.O. Box 244
Victoria
Tel. 22706

Boats can be hired for half or whole days from most of the big hotels and from:

Marine Charter Association
Avenue 5th June
Victoria
Tel. 22126
Telex 2359 MCA SZ

Game Fishing Club
Pirates Arms Hotel
P.O. Box 7
Victoria
Tel. 22939

Barralon's
Anse à la Mouche
Tel. 71069

Beau Vallon Bay Hotel
P.O. Box 550
Beau Vallon
Tel. 47141

Badminton, boccia, croquet

Badminton, boccia and croquet can be played at a number of hotels and also at the Seychelles College.

Golf

There are golf courses at the following hotels:
Reef Hotel (east coast of Mahé)
9 holes (open to non-residents)
Anse aux Pins
Tel. 76251;
Le Méridien–Barbarons Beach Hotel (west coast of Mahé)
9 holes (Beólière Country Golf)
Barbarons
Tel. 78253.
An 18-hole golf course is planned at Port Glaud.

Paragliding

There are facilities for paragliding on the beach at Beau Vallon Bay (Mahé) and on Thérèse Island.

Beau Vallon Aquatic Sports Centre
Beau Vallon Bay Hotel
Beau Vallon
Tel. 47141 ext. 825

Seyski Water Sports (Leisure 2000)
Coral Strand Hotel
Beau Vallon
Tel. 47036

Cycling

The best places for cycling are Praslin and La Digue. See Car and Bicycle Rental.

Horse riding

There are riding stables on the Barbarons Estates on the west coast of Mahé, with trekking in the wooded hills near by. Tel. 78577.

An Olympic swimming pool is being built (with Chinese aid) for the Indian Ocean Games in 1993.

Sailing and motor boats (also catamarans) can be hired bareboat or with crew on all the islands.

Boat hire companies on Mahé
Seychelles Yacht Club
P.O. Box 504
Avenue 5th June
Victoria
Tel. 22362
(Temporary membership available)

Marine Charter Association
Avenue 5th June
Victoria
Tel. 22126
Telex 2359 MCA SZ

Yacht Charter Company
P.O. Box 107
Tel. 78339
Telex 2201 SZ

Travel Services Seychelles
P.O. Box 356
Tel. 22414
Telex 2247 TRAVSY SZ

Seychelles Leisure Limited
P.O. Box 200
Tel. 23601

Boat hire companies on Praslin:
Indian Ocean Fishing Club
P.O. Box 393
Tel. 33324

Inter Island Cruising Pty. Ltd
c/o Maison des Palmes Hotel
Amitié
Tel. 33411
Telex 2326 PALMES SZ

There are squash courts at the École Polytechnique and at North East Point (Mahé).

In comparison with other Indian Ocean islands (or with the Antilles, Australian Great Barrier Reef or Red Sea for example) coral growth around the granite islands of the main Seychelles group is in many places sparse. In fact the "landscape" is much the same beneath the water as it is above. The great appeal of the Seychelles lies, rather, in the fish, particularly the larger species, with which the waters abound in numbers and a variety scarcely matched elsewhere. Most of the best diving grounds are in relatively small and circumscribed areas of open water far from the islands and locating them requires a good knowledge of the underwater topography. Much the best plan therefore is to go diving with a local guide.

Big sharks are usually only seen along the outer edges of the reef and in the deeper waters where the Mahé Plateau drops sharply away. Smaller varieties are found around the islands but will not ordinarily attack humans

unless provoked. The crevices and crannies in the granite of the underwater plateau provide the perfect environment for rays and nurse sharks,
as well as for turtles, crabs and spiny lobsters. The wreckage of the tanker
"Ennerdale", which sank off Mahé in 1970 and now lies scattered at depths
of between 8 and 32m (having been blown up by the British Navy), is a very
popular diving site. The waters of Cocos Island and Grand Anse on La
Digue are also much favoured by divers (see Diving Grounds).

Snorkellers should be sure to wear a T-shirt for protection against sunburn.

Diving trips (for which a diving certificate may be required) are organised
by local travel agents. Courses leading to a diving certificate are available
and can be taken while on holiday (the diving schools usually offer a free
introductory class in the hotel pool). Anyone enrolling for such a course
must be at least 16 years of age, physically fit and capable of swimming and
snorkelling. Most diving schools use the "PADI" system.

Diving courses and equipment hire on Mahé:
Marine Divers Seychelles
(Northholme Hotel)
P.O. Box 333
Victoria
Tel. 47589; Telex 2355 COSNOR SZ; Fax. 22753
Open: daily 9am–6pm

Beau Vallon Aquatic Sports Center
(Beau Vallon Bay Hotel)
Beau Vallon
Tel. 47141, ext. 825

Seychelles Underwater Centre
(Coral Strand Hotel)
P.O. Box 384
Beau Vallon
Tel. 47357; Telex 2215 CORAL SZ

Big Game Watersports
(Sheraton Hotel)
Port Glaud
Tel. 78451

Technosub
Rue Olivier Maradam
Victoria
Tel. 22078

Blue Lagoon Chalets
Anse à la Mouche
Tel. 71197

On Praslin:
Diving in Paradise
Praslin Beach Hotel
Anse Volbert
Tel. 32148

On La Digue:
La Morena Diving Centre
(La Digue Island Lodge)
Anse Réunion
Tel. 34233

On Desroches:
Windsurfing Seychelles, Desroches Watersports
P.O. Box 667/Mahé
Tel. 47230; Telex 2201 SZ

The calmer the water the better the conditions for diving, so the months from November to May are most favourable, especially in the Sainte Anne Marine National Park, some coastal areas of Mahé (Police Bay, Anse Royal Bay, Anse aux Pins) and Thérèse, also Silhouette, south-east Curieuse, Aride and Frégate. The two tranquil inter-monsoon periods are best for exploring the Ave Maria Rocks, the Ennerdale wreck, Anse Petit Cœur (Praslin), La Digue, Recifs and Bird Island. From June to September there is good diving off Beau Vallon Bay and Barbarons Beach (Mahé), La Digue (north-west side), Grande Sœur and Petite Sœur.

A number of Mahé's hotels (e.g. the Equator, Barbarons and Sheraton, Fisherman's Cove, Reef) have tennis courts, some floodlit. On Praslin there are courts at the Praslin Beach Hotel and on La Digue at La Réserve. Courts should be booked through the hotels. **Tennis**

There are one or two basic rules to be followed by anyone hill walking on the granite islands. Avoid walking at midday, it can become overpoweringly hot and humid. Always carry plenty to drink, even on supposedly short expeditions (hikes in mountainous terrain often take much longer than anticipated). Wear good strong shoes (not trainers!) and leave heavy, e.g. photographic equipment, behind. Keep away from the steeper and more challenging mountain paths in damp or misty weather. Remember too that a slower pace gives more opportunity for appreciating the landscape and the plants. **Walking**
Many of the tracks cut across private land. As a rule walkers are welcome, but any instructions from the landowner should of course be respected.

Windsurfing and water-skiing

The fire risk is great, particularly in the dry seasons, so never throw away cigarette ends or matches.

The tourist office will arrange guides for longer excursions on request (see Information).

A number of trails, graded according to difficulty, are described in "Suggested Routes and Walks" in the Introduction Section.

Windsurfing

Windsurfing is very popular in the Seychelles. Many hotels on Mahé, Praslin, La Digue, Desroches and Denis have surfboards for the use of guests (usually free, though a charge is made on Desroches) and/or offer courses for both beginners and the more experienced. Apart from the hotels there are also windsurfing schools on the beach at Beau Vallon Bay (Mahé).

Information:
Seychelles Windsurfing Pty. Ltd.
P.O. Box 667
Victoria
Tel. 23530

Taxis

General

Seychelles taxis are identified by a yellow stripe along the side. There are no taxi meters; instead, rates are fixed by the government and the official fares for the various routes are displayed in every taxi (if they are not displayed, ask to see them). Similar information can be obtained from hotels. Tipping is not customary, not even for longer periods of hire. There are also official fares for taxi tours which follow specified routes.

Mahé

Mahé has some 125 taxis providing a 24-hour service.
For information or to call a taxi: tel. 21703,
1–3am: tel. 47141

Information about day trips:
Taxi Association
Victoria
Tel. 23895

The following taxi ranks also take bookings:
Victoria: tel. 22279/23739/24199
Beau Vallon Bay Hotel: tel: 47499
Reef Hotel (Anse aux Pins): tel. 76509
Barbarons Beach Hotel: tel. 78629
International airport: tel. 73349
Harbour entrance: tel. 22239

Praslin

Praslin has about 15 taxis. Prices are 20% higher than on Mahé.

There are taxi ranks:
at the airport: tel. 33429
in Baie Ste Anne: tel. 33859

Telephone

See Post and Telephone

Tennis

See Sport

Theft

At one time theft was virtually unknown in the Seychelles. In recent years it has become more common, encouraged to some extent by the careless-ness with which some visitors leave valuables lying about on the beach, in open cars, or unlocked hotel rooms. Articles of value should be deposited in the hotel safe where they are at least insured. Parking one of the popular Mini Mokes at the beach with belongings inside is asking for trouble – there is absolutely no way of locking them.

Time

Seychelles time is four hours ahead of GMT, three hours ahead of British Summer Time. On Denis Island, which observes its own time, clocks are advanced a further hour.

Tipping

Hotels and restaurants generally include a service charge in the bill; a tip of between 3 and 5% is normally added. If, however, a menu has a special note on it, satisfied customers leave a tip of about 10%. Small tips are also customary for other services – e.g. R 1 for a porter and a sum equivalent to Rs 2 or 3 per day for the chambermaid.

Traffic Regulations

Vehicles travel on the left in the Seychelles. In Victoria and the other settlements and villages the speed limit is 40kph; outside built-up areas it is 60kph. On Praslin there is a single limit of 40kph. In most other respects the traffic regulations in force are the familiar international ones. Foreign drivers must be over 21 years old and must carry with them a national or international driving licence.

Road signs are generally poor and often lacking altogether. The police posts seen at many crossroads are clearly identified however and can be a useful aid to finding the way.

Transport

See Air Travel, Boat Services, Buses, Taxis.

Travel Documents

All visitors to the Seychelles must be in possession of a valid passport, and on arrival are issued with a one-month visa. Extensions to the visa for a further month, or for periods up to a year, can be obtained on application to the local immigration authorities (Principal Immigration Officer, P.O. Box 430, Mahé, Seychelles) provided proof is forthcoming of adequate financial means.

A national driving licence is recognised for the period of the holiday.   Driving licence

Walking

See Sport

When to go

As the islands are situated close to the equator, the weather in the Seychelles is always pleasantly warm and suitable for holidays at any time of
year. For further details see Climate and the climatic table in the Introduction Section.

Windsurfing

See Sport

Index

Index